KEEPAHEAD PRESS
ARCHITECTURAL THEORY SERIES

The series offers texts that are significant for an understanding of the history of architecture but that are presently out of print or not available in English translations.

1. Heinrich Wölfflin, *Prolegomenon to a Psychology of Architecture* (1886). German text, and English translation by Michael Selzer. Paperback $12.50. ISBN 13:978-1541071674

2. August Thiersch, *Proportion in Architecture* (1883). With 70 illustrations from the original edition. English translation by Michael Selzer. Paperback $12.50. ISBN 13: 978-1542769457

3. Roland Freart, sieur de Chambray, *A Parallel of the Antient Architecture with the Modern in a Collection of Ten Principal Authors who have written upon the Five Orders...* Translation by John Evelyn (1664). *Forthcoming,* 2017.

Prolegomena to a Psychology of Architecture

Prolegomena

zu einer

Psychologie der Architektur.

INAUGURAL-DISSERTATION

der

hohen philosophischen Fakultät
der Universität München

zur Erlangung

der höchsten akademischen Würden

vorgelegt von

Heinrich Wölfflin.

München, 1886.

Kgl. Hof- & Universitäts-Buchdruckerei von Dr. C. Wolf & Sohn.

Title page of Wolfflin's dissertation,
University of Munich, 1886

Heinrich Wölfflin

Prolegomena to a Psychology of Architecture

Translated by Michael Selzer

KeepAhead Books
Colorado Springs, 2017

Also by Michael Selzer from KeepAhead Press

The Symmetry Norm and the Asymmetric Universe
Footnotes from a Bookseller's Life
Renewing the Fear, A Jew goes to Berlin
Snuffing up the Wind. Theomonarchism in the Biblical Text

To the memory of
Florence R. Miale
1916-1990

ISBN-13: 978-1541071674
ISBN-10: 1541071670

10 9 8 7 6 5 4 3 2

Table of Contents

German Text

Translator's Note

This is at least the third translation into English of Wölfflin's dissertation. I have not seen the earliest of these, which was published by MIT's architecture department in 1976; copies of it are listed in Worldcat only at libraries at MIT and Harvard. In 1994 Mallgrave and Ikonomou's translation appeared in their collection of late 19th-century German aesthetic writing published by the Getty Center.[1] This is a reliable translation, for the most part, and it is garnished by the translation of corrections that Wölfflin made at a later date in the margins of his own copy of the text. (The more significant of these are included here as footnoted "HW marginal notes" in square brackets.) This edition has long been out of print, however, and the few copies on the market are, to say the least, excessively expensive, being offered at anywhere from $490 to $1150.

In the view of Alina Payne, an art historian, Wölfflin's *Prolegomena* is a "lucid and powerful" work.[2] Many who read it, however, are more likely to sympathize with the opinion of Joan Golhammer Hart that the text, for all its brevity, is "not a coherent whole", that Wölfflin's ideas are often "bizarre and puzzling" and his arguments

---

[1] Mallgrave, Harry Francis and Eleftherios Ikonomou: *Empathy, Form, and Space.Problems in German Aesthetics 1987-1893.* Santa Monica, CA: Getty Center for the History of Art and the Humanities, 1994.

[2] Payne, Aline: *From Ornament to Object. Genealogies of Architectural Modernism.* New Haven and London: Yale University Press, 2012, p. 116

"tenuous".

As if to warn off foolhardy translators, moreover, Hart also states that the work is written "in almost outline, with terse sentences" and that its style alone "could create a barrier to understanding". Most ominously, she writes that the text is "full of undefined and equivalent terms".[3] To help readers cope with them – and perhaps to shift the burden from my weak shoulders! – I give the German of Wölfflin's more elusive terms in italicized parentheses. Those inclined to do so may seek to determine their meaning from the original text, which comprises the second half of this volume. I should add here that I have attempted to penetrate, rather than to convey the tone of, Wölfflin's frequently turgid 19th-century academic prose. This has been done, I believe, without significantly distorting the meaning of the text, though I must acknowledge that there are a few short passages whose meaning I have had to guess from the context.

With all its shortcomings, however, Wölfflin's *Prolegomena* is nevertheless a notable achievement, whose scope and authority are astonishing for a work written before its author reached the age of 22. Although reflecting the ideas of a number of prominent writers of the day – who are now perhaps remembered chiefly for their influence on Wölfflin – it advanced in a notable manner the application of psychological insights to the understanding of how we perceive art. Few of those insights have stood the test of time, it is true, and his understanding of "psychology" is hopelessly obsolete; but

---

[3] Hart, Joan Goldhammer: *Heinrich Wölfflin: An Intellectual Biography,* unpublished Ph.D. dissertation, U. of Cal. Berkeley, 1981, pp. 2, 21.

Wölfflin's basic thesis, that it is through our awareness of our own bodies that we are able to become aware of the expressiveness of buildings, remains valid and useful.[4]

Michael Selzer

---

[4] Notable discussions of Wölfflin's *Prolegomena* include the works already cited by Mallgrave and Ikonomou, and by Hart; also, Rudolf Arnheim, "Confessions of a Maverick", *Salmagundi* No.7/9, (1988); Marshall Brown, "The Classic in the Baroque: on the Principles of Wolfflin's Art History", *Critical Inquiry* v.9 (1982); Richard Etlin, "Aesthetics of the Spatial Sense of Self", *J. of Aesthetics* v.56 (1998); and Juliet Koss, "On the Limits of Empathy", *Art Bulletin* v.88 (2006). On Wölfflin's treatment of the concept of symmetry, see my *The Symmetry Norm and the Asymmetric Universe*, Colorado Springs: Keep Ahead Press, 4th ed., (forthcoming, 2017).

Foreword

The observations presented here address the question, one that has always struck me as most remarkable, of how it is that architectural Forms are able to express emotions and moods.

There is no doubting the fact itself. It is not only confirmed by the layman's strongly-held opinion that every building conveys a distinctive impression, from the serious and gloomy, to the cheerful and friendly – a whole range of moods: but also by the art historian, who does not hesitate to characterize entire periods and nations by their architecture. The expressiveness of buildings is therefore acknowledged. But how? On what principles does the historian base his judgements?

I am surprised that there are virtually no answers to such questions in the scholarly literature. A great deal of care and love have been devoted to studying the analogous problem in music, but architecture has not received similar attention from either psychology or art theory. I make this point, not by way of claiming to fill in this gap myself but rather to provide myself with an excuse for my effort here. T

The reader should not expect more than an outline. What I present here are merely prolegomena to a psychology of architecture that has yet to be written. For what is often only a suggestive handling of the topic, I must justify myself by reference to the title.

1. Psychological Foundation

The task of the psychology of architecture is to describe and explain the emotions that the art of building is able, with its resources, to arouse.

We call the effects of those emotions on us *impressions*.

And we consider these impressions to be *expressions* of objects.

Accordingly, we can formulate the problem as:

How can architectural Forms be expressions?

(Under "architectural Forms" we must also consider the lesser arts of decoration and handicrafts, for they are affected by the same conditions of expression.)

We can try to answer this question from two sides – from the subjective side and from the objective side.

Both have been done.

I will mention first the well-known theory that explains the emotional tone of a form by the muscle sense (*Muskelgefühl*) of the eye as it follows a line. Our feelings for a wavy line are substantially different from those for a zigzag.

In what way are they different?

It is said that the movement of the eye as it traces a line is easier in the one case than it is in the other. "When the eye moves freely its physiological structure enables it to move in an exactly straight line in both vertical and horizontal directions, but when it moves in any oblique direction it does so in an arc." (Wundt, *Vorlesungen*, II:80)

This explains our pleasure in the wavy line and our dislike of the zigzag. The beauty of a form is a function of its suitability for our eye. We can express the same idea by pointing out that the purpose of a column's capital is to lead the eye gradually from the vertical to the horizontal, or that the contour of a mountain is beautiful because the eye is able to glide smoothly and without hesitation over it.

The theory sounds reasonable enough, perhaps, when presented in these terms, but it fails the necessary test of experience. One asks oneself how much of a form's actual impression is explained by the muscle sense of the eye. Is the greater or lesser ease with which the eye moves really the essential determinant of the multiplicity of effects it perceives? Even the most superficial psychological analysis must show how little reality is to be found in this idea. In fact, one cannot even grant it a secondary role. Noting very correctly that equal pleasure can be had from a wavy line as from a right-angled meander, Lotze points out that no physical effort is involved in making aesthetic judgments, and that aesthetic pleasure is not determined by the ease with which we make those judgments. (*Geschichte der Aesthetik in Deutschland*, p.310 *f.*)

The quite obvious error here seems to be the assumption that because the *eye* perceives physical forms it is their visible features that determine what their characteristics are. But the eye seems to react with pleasure or lack of pleasure only to the intensity of light. It is indifferent to forms, or at least is absolutely unable to identify their expressive qualities.

We must therefore look for another principle. We will find it in the comparison with music. There we have the same relationship. The ear is the perceiving organ, but we could never experience the emotional content of sounds by analyzing auditory processes. In order to understand the theory of musical expression we need to observe *one's own creation of sounds*, the meaning and use of *our own vocal instrument.*

Had we lacked the ability to express our own feelings with sounds we would never ever understand the meaning of others' sounds. One understands only what one can do oneself.

So here too we must say: *Physical forms only have characteristics because we ourselves have physical form.* If we were beings who only perceived things visually, an aesthetic judgement of the physical world would always be denied us. However, as human beings with bodies that teach us to know what gravity, contraction, strength and so on are, we acquire the experiences that first enable us to empathize with the conditions of external forms. Why does no one marvel at the fact that the stone falls to the ground: why does that strike us as so very natural? We have no trace of a rational understanding of such an occurrence, the explanation lies solely in our own experience. We have carried loads and have experienced what pressures and counter-pressures are, and we have sunk to the ground when we no longer have the strength to counter the downward-pulling weight of our own bodies, and that is why we know how to value the proud fortune of a column and understand the tendency of all Matter to spread out formlessly on the ground.

One could say that this has no bearing on the understanding of *linear* and *planimetric* relationships, but that objection is based on faulty observation. As soon as one pays attention, one finds that one attributes a mechanical meaning to such relationships too, that there is no oblique line that we do not perceive as rising and no irregular triangle that we do not perceive as deprived of balance. It hardly needs to be said that architectural structures are not merely geometric but have the effect of *massive forms* (*Massenformen*). But that is a premise that is put forward repeatedly by proponents of an extreme formal aesthetics.

We can go further. Musical sounds would have no meaning if we did not regard them as the expression of some kind of sensitive being. This relationship, which was natural to the original musical form, namely song, has been obscured but not abolished by instrumental music. We always associate sounds we hear to a subject whose expression they are.

And so it is in the physical world. Forms acquire meaning for us only because we recognize in them the expression of a sentient (*fühlend*) soul. Spontaneously, we animate (*beseelen*) every object. That is a basic instinct in man. It is the origin of mythological imagination and, even today, does it not require a prolonged educational process to free ourselves of the impression that a figure whose balance is disturbed cannot have a sense of well-being? Will this instinct ever die out? I believe not. It would be the death of art.

We project the image of our selves onto everything we see. What we know to be the conditions of our own well-being we expect everything else to possess. It is not that we demand to see a human shape in the forms of inorganic nature, but that we perceive the material world through the categories (if I may put it this way) that we have in common with it. The expressive potential of these alien forms, too, becomes apparent in this way. *They can only communicate to us what we ourselves express with their traits.*

Here, some will become skeptical and will doubt whether there are similarities or any expressive feelings that we share with dead stone. I will say it briefly: there are varying quantities of heaviness, of balance, of hardness, etc., that all have expressive value for us. All that pertains to humanity, naturally, can only be expressed through that which is human, and so architecture cannot express specific emotions that are manifested in particular organs. Nor should it try to do so. Its object remains *the great existential feelings*, the emotions that posit the stable and constant condition of the body.

I could finish this section now and at most point out how language too provides an abundance of examples showing that unconquerable propensity of our imagination for perceiving everything in the physical world in the form of living beings. We can remind ourselves of architectural terminology. Wherever a circumscribed entity puts in an appearance, we give it a head and foot, look for its front and rear, and so on.

Yet there still remains the question of how the vivifying (*beseelung*) of these alien forms should be con-ceptualized. There is not likely to be a satisfactory answer to this, but I do not want to ignore it because it is a goal that has been approached from other angles.

The anthropomorphic conception of three-dimensional structures is not unheard-of. In modern aesthetics this is the process that has come to be known as *symbolizing*.

Johann Volkelt[5] has written the history of the term "symbol", which brought him much merit by its more exact version of what had originally been suggested by Herder[6] and Lotze.[7]

---

[5] Volkelt, *Symbolbegriff in her neueren Ästhetik*, Jena 1876.
[6] "Kalligone", as well as the essay "Plastik", contain notable comments.
[7] Lotze, *Geschichte der Ästhetik in Deutchland; and Microcosmos*, v.II, 198ff.

In Volkelt's view the symbolization of three-dimensional structures is carried out in the following ways (*Symbolbegriff,* 51-70):

1. The three-dimensional structure is construed in terms of movement and the effect of forces, a process that should not be called symbolic: in tracing the contours of things we see, we enliven the lines so that they flow and run.

2. To understand the three-dimensional structure aesthetically we must experience this movement with our senses by accompanying it with our bodily organization.

3. A feeling of pleasure and pain is bound up with the stretching and movement of our bodies; we understand it as characteristic of the natural form itself.

4. To be called aesthetic, however, this feeling of pleasure must have a mental significance: the bodily movement and the physical sensation must be the expression of a sentiment.

5. The fact that our entire being participates in aesthetic pleasure indicates that all such pleasure must contain something of human nature in general, something of the idea that constitutes a human being.

So much for Volkelt's analysis.

I am essentially in complete agreement with it. The objections that could be raised against Point 1 and against the separation of Points 3 and 4 can be disregarded here. I want to focus all the attention on the core of the thing, to the second point: the empathic experiencing of the external form. How might we "enter the object with our bodily feeling"? Volkelt intentionally keeps us in the dark on this point, and later finds (along with *Fr. Vischer*) the only solution in a pantheistic conception of the world. He does not want to approach this process, filled as it is with arcana, too closely: "With my vital feeling I lay myself darkly into the object", he says (p.61), and elsewhere he speaks of "transporting oneself", and so on. To be sure, one cannot uncover the entire course of this psychic act, yet I want to ask, "Is this experience a *sensory* one, or does it only take place in the imagination?" In other words, do we experience outside physical forms with our own bodies?

Or: is our empathy with those forms only a function of our imagination?

Volkelt wavers here. Sometimes he says that we must experience the object *sensually* with our physical organization (p. 57), but on other occasions that it is only the imagination that carries out the movement (pp. 61-62).

Lotz and Rob. Vischer[8], who were the first to assert the relevance of bodily experience, were clearly only thinking of processes that take place in the imagination. In this sense, according to Rob. Vischer: "We possess the wonderful ability to project and merge our own physical form into an objective form". Similarly, Lotze: "No form is so impermeable that our imagination is unable to mix its living self into it".

If I understand correctly, Volkelt has gone further here than his predecessors, without however under-standing the problem more exactly.

There can be no doubt about the legitimacy of the question. For the physical affect that we experience when we observe an architectural work is undeniable. I can well

---

[8] Rob. Vischer, *Das optische Formengefühl.* Leipzig, 1872.

believe that someone could make the claim that the impression of a mood conveyed by architecture consists alone of this, that we involuntarily seek to simulate alien forms through our physical organization: in other words, we judge the existential feeling of architectural forms by the physical responses we make to them. Powerful columns arouse us with nervous energy, our breathing responds to the width or the narrowness of a three-dimensional space. We are energized as if we were the supporting columns, and breathe as deeply and fully as if our chest were as broad as this hall. Asymmetry often induces in us a feeling of physical pain, as if one of our limbs were missing, or injured, and in the same way we feel discomfort at the sight of a disturbed equilibrium – and so on. Everyone will recall similar instances in his own experience. And when Goethe sometimes says that one should be able to sense the effect of a beautiful room even if led through it blindfolded, he was expressing nothing other than the same thought: that the impression made by architecture, far from being something like a "visual tallying", essentially consists of an unmediated bodily feeling.

Instead of some incomprehensible "projection of the self" we could perhaps imagine that impulses from the optic nerve directly stimulate the motor nerves and cause the contraction of specific muscles. We could offer as a helpful analogy the fact that a musical note will make all related notes resonate, too.

What might the proponent of such an opinion say?

He might well cite the human transmission of expressiveness, or the theory which has recently been proposed that the understanding of human expression is mediated by empathy.

From which the following axioms can be formulated;

1. Every mood has its specific expression that regularly accompanies it; for an expression is not only a banner, as it were, hung out to show what is going on inside, nor is it something that might just as well not be there. Expression, rather, is the physical manifestation of a mental process. It is not only found in the tension of facial muscles or in the movements of the extremities, but extends itself to the entire organism.

2. No sooner does one imitate the expression of an emotion than one immediately experiences the emotion itself. Suppressing the expression is to suppress the emotion. On the other hand, giving in to it by expressing it causes it to grow all the more. The fearful person becomes more fearful if he expresses his anxiety in gestures.

3. One can often see someone unconsciously imitating another person's expressions and, in doing so, transferring emotions. One knows how children abandon them-selves unrestrainedly to any strong impression: they cannot see someone cry, for example, without their own tears starting to fall, and so on. Only in instances when they energetically express their own feelings

are they blocked from such responses, for empathy like this implies a certain degree of lack of will. Later on, education and rational reflection lead one not to give in to every impression. But at certain moments one "forgets oneself" and acts in a way that would make sense only if one were the other person.

Instances in which people project themselves include the following:

Someone with a hoarse throat tries to talk. We clear our own throat. Why? Because in that instant we believe that we ourselves are hoarse and want to free ourselves from that (or at least, to reassure ourselves of the clarity of our own voice.)

Moreover, it often happens during a painful operation that we exactly mimic the features of the sufferer, even to the extent of experiencing acute pain in the affected area.

These are unusual cases, to be sure, and one cannot deny that in the fleeting moments of daily life physical empathy has vanished almost without trace and that we accept the forms in which our fellow men express themselves as we do copper tokens whose valu we know from experience. Yet a stimulus remains, even if the impressed expression – if I may put it that way – does not rise to the surface (making itself apparent in face and posture). For the *inner organs* above all will be sympathetically aroused, and it is my observation that it is the *breathing* that is most easily altered. The rhythm of breathing that we observe in others is most readily transferred to ourselves. It is horrifying to see someone suffocate, for we can feel the torment of it, while we remain unmoved by the sight of a person's physical pain. This is an important fact, for it is precisely the breath that is the most direct organ of expression.

This is how an advocate of the idea of physical empathy might introduce his evidence, also hoping thereby perhaps to find support in the fact that conformity to the rule is experienced unconsciously by the intellect, or, on the contrary, that a breach of normality strikes the "eye" or the "feelings" (as we are accustomed to say) before the intellect detects *where* the error lies.

If someone wants to interject that empathy is irrelevant to aesthetic perception, because the imitation of human physiognomic expression only takes place involuntarily, in moments in which one *forgets oneself* and sinks oneself entirely in the object, this objection can be refuted by the absolutely correct observation that it is precisely this absence of will, this surrender of self-awareness, that is demanded for aesthetic perception.

Whoever is unable to stop thinking about himself for a while will never enjoy a work of art, let alone be able to create one.[9]

Even proponents of this thesis must acknowledge that the *sublime* evokes no such imitative response. While a well-lit colonnade with its buoyant strength infuses us with a direct sense of wellbeing, the sublime, by contrast, brings out the symptoms of fear. We feel the impossibility of relating to its immensity (*Ungeheuren*), the limbs

---

[9] Note. It is on this psychological fact that the relationship between moral and intellectual states of mind is based. The "compassion" that the one presupposes is psychologically the same process as aesthetic empathy. That is why great artists are well known to be always "good people", that is, subject in a high degree to feelings of compassion.

weaken, *and so on.* But the sublime is exceptional and is by no means rebuttal of the main point.

No one can contest our right to liken the perception of human expression to the perception of architectural forms. Where is the point at which this experience of empathy ceases? It will occur wherever we find existential conditions similar to our own, that is, where *bodies* confront us.

This inquiry, if pursued further, would return us to the mysteries of the history of psychological evolution. And even if we could eventually confirm a universal experience, if we could prove that our bodies undergo exactly the changes that correspond to the expression of a sentiment that the object communicates to us – what would that accomplish?

Who can tell us which has priority? Is the bodily affect a prerequisite for the impression of a mood? Or are the sensory feelings merely the product of a vivid imagination? Or finally, a third possibility, do the psychological and the bodily run parallel to each other?

Since we have driven the question to this point, it is high time to break it off: for we now face problems that mark the limits of all science.

We pull back. In what follow we will pay no attention to these difficulties, but will use the convenient traditional expressions that are at hand.

The foundation that has been laid is this:

Our bodily organization is the medium through which we experience everything physical. I will now show that the basic elements of architecture – material and form, gravity and force, are defined by the experiences that we have had of ourselves; that the laws of formal aesthetics are none other than the conditions under which alone organic well - being seems possible; and last, that the expression inherent in horizontal and vertical structuring (*Gliederung*) is constituted according to human (organic) principles.

This is the content of the ensuing sections.

I am far indeed from claiming that the architectural impression is completely analyzed in this way, for many other factors are certainly involved: color, associations that grow out of the history and the function of a building, the nature of the material, etc. Yet I do not think I am mistaken in seeing the essence of that impression in the outline presented here.

Disregarding these other factors, allow me to point to what one might call *analogies of linear awareness.*

By analogies of awareness Wundt (*phys. Psych* 1: 486ff) understands the connections that we tend to perceive between sensations of the different senses: for example, those between low notes and dark colors which, when considered purely as sensations have nothing in common, but seem related to each other by their identical somber emotional tone.

Such analogies are also present in lines. It would be desirable, for once, to hear something coherent about this completely overlooked subject.[10] I will make a few observations that were derived from numerous experiments.

The abrupt thrusts of the zigzag immediately bring to mind a burning red, while a soft blue suggests a gentle, wavy line; a paler shade suggests a long drawn-out

---

[10] Naturally, linguistic research must support the experimental psychologist in this regard.

wave, a stronger shade a more sprightly one. And indeed the word "faint" is used both for colors lacking in intensity and for physical fatigue.[11]

Similarly, we speak of warm and cold lines,[12] of the warm lines of a woodcut, for instance, and the cold ones of the steel engraving: opposites that correspond to sensations of hard and soft pressures.

This is clearest in the analogy with musical sounds, where perhaps the experience of creating sounds with our own voices plays a part. Everyone regards a line with short, small waves as a vibrato on a high register, and wide, shallow undulations as a muffled buzz. The zigzag "rattles and clatters like gunfire" (Jakob Burckhardt); a very pointy line has the effect of a piercing whistle. The straight line is altogether silent.

It therefore makes good sense, with regard to architecture, to speak of the *quiet* simplicity of antiquity and the unpleasant clamor of, for example, English Gothic. Or perhaps in the gently receding lines of a mountain we experience a softly fading sound.

2. The Subject of Architecture

Matter is heavy, its thrusts downwards, and wants to spread itself formlessly on the ground. We know the force of gravity from our own bodies. What keeps us upright, and averts a formless collapse? It is the opposing force that we can identify as will, life, or whatever. I call

---

[11] [HW marginal note:] "Colors. Dull colors. See the muted colors of Roman Baroque and the strong Venetian coloring and their correspondingly different architecture. Gothic: harsh colors. Rococo: light, muted, *bleu mourant.*"

[12] [HW marginal note:] "This is nonsense".

it Form Force [*Formkraft*]. *The opposition of Matter and Form Force*, which moves the entire organic world, is the basic theme of architecture. Aesthetic perception even infuses this most intimate experience of our bodies into lifeless nature. We suppose that in everything there is a will that attempts to become form and must overcome the opposition of formless Matter.

With this recognition we have taken the decisive step, both to augment formal aesthetics with propositions that are more vital, and to ensure that the architectural impression has richer content than is accorded to it in, for example, *Schopenhauer's* celebrated theory. Fortunately, no one allows philosophy to dampen their pleasure, and Schopenhauer himself had too much artistic sensitivity to believe his own proposition that gravity and rigidity are the only subject-matter of architecture.

Because he analyzed neither the impression nor the psychological impact of architecture, but only its material substance, he let himself be led to the conclusion that:

1. Art expresses the ideas of Nature.
2. The main ideas of architectural Matter are gravity and rigidity.
3. Accordingly, the task of Art is to present these ideas clearly in their contradiction of one another.

The load wishes to fall to the ground; the supports, by virtue of their rigidity, oppose this wish.

Aside from the intellectual weakness of this juxtaposition, it is hard to understand how Schopenhauer could have been blind to the fact that our aesthetic perception completely sets aside the rigidity of the stone of a Greek column and converts it into a vital reaching up to the heights.

Enough. I repeat: just as the character of gravity is inferred from our physical experiences, without which it would be inconceivable to us, so too do we apprehend that which opposes gravity with a human, which is to say an organic, analog. And so I hold that all the axioms of formal aesthetics concerning *beautiful forms* are nothing other than *the prerequisites of organic life.* Form Force, accordingly is not only the antithesis of gravity, a force that works vertically, but that which brings forth life, a *vis plastica*, to use an expression disdained in the Natural Sciences. In the next section I will state the individual laws of form. Here, it will be sufficient to suggest the basic idea, which is the relation of Matter and Form.

After all that has been said there should be no doubt that Form is not an external thing that is thrown over Matter, but that it is, rather, something that works its way out of Matter, as immanent Will; Matter and Form are inseparable. In all Matter there lives a Will that seeks Form, but cannot always attain it. One should also not imagine that Matter is the unconditional enemy, for Matter-less Form is inconceivable; every- where, the image of our physical existence presents itself as the type by which we gauge all visual phenomena. Matter is the evil principle only insofar as we encounter it as life-threatening gravity. The effects of gravity are always bound up with lessening of vital energy. Blood flows more slowly, breathing becomes irregular and gasping; the body loses its support and collapses. These are the moments of loss of balance, and gravity seems to overpower us. Language has expressions for this: *gloom, depressed* moods, etc. I will not try to determine further what disturbances of a physical nature are present here: enough to say that this is the condition of *Formlessness*.

Everything living seeks to escape its grasp, and to attain a natural bearing of regularity and balance. In this attempt by organic Will to penetrate the body, the relationship of Form to Matter is made apparent.

To some degree Matter itself yearns for Form. And so one can describe this process with the same words that Aristotle used for the relationship of his Forms to Matter, or with Goethe's marvelous expression, "the image must work its way out". The completed Form however presents itself as an entelechy, as the consummation of what was potential in Matter.

All these resemblances, basically, rest on the deeply human experience of forming that which is unformed. In desciding architecture as frozen music, one is only expressing the idea that both arts have the same effect on us. While the rhythmic waves penetrate us, grip us, and draw us into the beautiful movement, everything formless dissipates and we have the good fortune to be free for a moment from the down-thrusting gravity of Matter.

We feel a similar formative force in all archi-tectural creations, except that it does not come from outside but from within as formative Will that generates its own body. The objective is not the destruction of Matter but only the organic construction of it, a condition that we perceive is self-willed, not the result of external force; *self-determination* is the prerequisite of all beauty. That the weight of Matter has been overcome, that in the most powerful masses a Will that is *intelligible to us* has been able to fulfill itself: this is the fundamental essence of the architectural impression.

Realizing the potential, fulfilling the Will, liberation from material gravity – these expressions all mean the same thing.

The greater the resistance that is overcome, the greater the delight.

Now, what matters is not merely that a Will is fulfilled, but what kind of Will it is. A cube completely satisfies the first condition, but its content is very meager.

In formally-correct, that is, viable, architecture a development is possible that one would not be unjustified in likening to the development of organic entities. Both progress similarly from vague, slightly-differentiated parts to the most finely formed system of differentiated parts.

Architecture reaches its apogee at the point where, from the undifferentiated mass, individual organs detach themselves and each part appears to function in accordance with its own purpose alone, and without affecting the entire body or being obstructed by it.

The same objective is pursued by Nature in its organic structures. The lowest beings form an unarticulated whole; necessary functions are either performed by "pseudo-organs" that occasionally emerge from the mass and then disappear into it again, or that possess one organ alone to serve all functions but that does so in a very cumbersome way. The highest beings, on the other hand, display a system of differentiated parts that are able to function independently of one another. To fully develop this independence requires practice. The fresh recruit, at first, cannot march without involving his whole body, the piano student cannot raise one finger alone.

The discomfort that such conditions give rise to, when the Will is unable to prevail, when it it is stuck in Matter, is the same feeling that we get from insufficiently differentiated buildings. (The Romanesque style has abundant examples of this kind.)

Because the greater autonomy of the parts indicates the greater perfection of the organism, a creature becomes more meaningful to us the more dissimilar its parts are to one another (within the limits, of course, laid down by the general laws of Form: see the next section). The Gothic, in whose parts the same pattern is always repeated: tower = *pinnacle,* gabel = *hood*, an unending multiplicity of identical and similar parts, is inferior to antiquity, which repeats nothing: *one* order, *one* entablature, *one* pediment.

I shall break off these observations. They can be productive only when the architectural organism is already known in all its parts. What I had wanted to show is only that we assess the perfection of an architectural creation by the same criterion that we use for living creatures.

We turn now to the general laws of Form.

3. Form and its Aspects

In order to have a strong foundation I will take as the determinants of Form those that Fr. Vischer gives in his self-critique of his work on aesthetics (*Krit. Gänge* V).

He differentiates two external and four internal aspects.

The first are:

1.Demarcation of space

2.Measure, relative to the vigor of our
   visual perception (not essential to
   us here).

It is *conditio sine qua non* that each thing, in order to be individual, must create a boundary between itself and its surroundings. This type of demarcation will be discussed presently.

   The inner aspects are:
   1.Regularity
   2.Symmetry
   3.Proportion
   4.Harmony

To develop these concepts, I will begin by taking for a motto, as it were, the basic principle that has already been laid down: The aspects of Form are nothing other than the conditions of organic existence and as such have no meaning for expressions. They present only a model of that which is alive (*Schema des Lebendigen*).

   Regularity is defined as "the uniform repetition of different but similar parts". Vischer names as examples: an order of columns, the sequence of a decorative pattern, the straight line, the circle, the square, etc.

   Here I think I must first criticize an inaccuracy. The *regularity* of an array must clearly be distinguished from the "*lawfulness*" of a line such as a straight line, of a figure such as a square or a circle, or – according to linguistic usage – also a 90-degree angle as opposed to one of 80 degrees.

   It is not clear how one definition can embrace all these things.

   The difference between regularity and what I have for the time being referred to as lawfulness is based on a very profound difference: *Here* we have before us a pure *intellectual* relationship; *there,* a *physical* one. The lawfulness that expresses itself in an angle of 90 degrees or in a square has no connection to our organism, it does not please us as an attractive vital form, it is no universal organic condition of life, but only something that is favored by our intellect. The regularity of a sequence, on the other hand, is to us something that we find valuable, because our organism's structure demands regularity in its functions. We breathe regularly, we walk regularly, and every ongoing activity is performed in a periodic sequence. Another example: a pyramid ascends at exactly 45 degrees, offering us merely intellectual pleasure, our organism is indifferent to it, for it reckons merely with the relationship of force and gravity and passes its judgment on that basis.

It is important to make the principal difference between these two factors as clear as possible.

They can almost never be observed in total isolation, for every intellectual relationship also has some physical meaning, and *vice versa.* Yet it is usually not difficult to detect each in the combination of parts.

The intellectual factor has almost no meaning at all for the character, that is to say, for the expression, of a work of art. After all, an easily recognizable order will increase the appeal of its serenity, while by contrast a very complex and intellectually impenetrable arrangement seems to take on a character of dull annoyance in which we become displeased as the result of the failure of our effort. Where the intention is all too readily discerned the result is usually a dull, boring impression.

The intellectual factor is important only in the formal sense, because it guarantees the *self-determination* of an object. Where we find strict rules and understandable quantities, there we know that chance has not triumphed, that this form is willed, and this object is self-determined (naturally, this can only occur within the limits of physical possibility). It is an interesting point that the earliest art, which aimed above all to replace the haphazard forms of nature with intentional shapes, believed that this goal could only be attained by crude rules. It was reserved for a later age to convey an impression of inevitability specifically through freer forms.

Symmetry. Vischer defines it as a "juxtaposition of identical parts around a separate and dissimilar middle point". One can perhaps accept this so long as one is clear that nothing further need be said other than that the sides to the right and left of the *given* center must be the same. As it stands, the definition leads one to the belief that this concept also includes the *establishment* of a center, which is altogether incorrect, for where it is not present, for example in ordinarily regular forms, one does not talk of asymmetry.

The demand for symmetry is derived from the arrangement of our bodies. Because we are built symmetrically, we believe that we are entitled to demand this form for all architectural bodies, too. And this, not because we regard our species as the most beautiful, as people often think, but because it alone seems right to us.

The effect of asymmetry, as has already been noted, makes the relationship clear: we feel physical discomfort. Because we have identified ourselves in a symbolic way with the object, it is for us as if the symmetry of our own body has been disturbed, or as if a limb were mangled.

The unchallengeable value of the demand for symmetry stems from its origins. One often encounters the opinion that it (symmetry) must at once yield to utility without its appeal suffering any loss. Fechner (*Vorschule der Aesthetik)* gives the example of a cup that has only one handle. It is just here, however, that we can best validate our principle. Even without thinking about it we make the side with the handle be the *rear* of the cup, so that the symmetry is preserved. But if there are two handles, the relationship changes again and we regard it as analogous to our arms.

All this, however, suffices to show that expressiveness is not inherent in symmetry as such, any more than the similarity of a person's arms arouses one's emotions.

Proportion causes greater difficulties. It is an entirely undeveloped concept. *Vischer's* definition - proportion posits inequality and prescribes an order that dominates it - does not say much, as he himself acknowledges. Adding that it holds true of the vertical direction contributes nothing, for it then no longer applies to surfaces (the relationship of height to width) where one also speaks of proportion. And just as with height and width one can also say: beams must be proportional to their load.

From all these instances one sees only one thing: it is about the relationship of different parts to one another. If they are called *force* and *load* then only function can decide: and the beam must be measured for its load - that is obvious, a physical principle.

Further, height and width must stand in a "relationship" to one another, 1:1, 1:2, the Golden Section are such relationships, but I will first address them in the section on the expressive value of proportion. The question does not belong here because it lacks any consistent, necessary and thus expression-less form.

Finally, to take a numerical order as the main principle of vertical composition is entirely inappropriate, for there is a *qualitative* aspect here: the modeling of the load-bearing [*widerstrebenden*] material from bottom to top. With symmetry the parts were qualitatively the same. Here, the lower parts are the heavy and compressed; the upper, the light and more finely fashioned. Numerical ratios, such as the Golden Section (over-valued by Zeising), come in here as somewhat secondary, but above all we demand to see this qualitative progression expressed from bottom to top.

The laws of this progression defy mathematical definition. A rusticated ground floor of the same height as the second floor above it with a *smooth* wall does not function as 1:1, for with dissimilar materials the visual surfaces no longer decide the matter.

Here too the principle is borrowed from organic structures. We find this evolution from the raw to the refined most completely in human beings. Wundt (*Phys. Psych.* II, 186) notes that a repetition of homologous parts takes place, "in the arms and hands the legs and feet are repeated in finer and more complete form. Similarly, the chest repeats the form of the stomach. But where all the other parts are repeated just twice in the vertical structuring of the form, on top of them in the section on the expressive value of proportion. The question does not belong here because it lacks any consistent, necessary and thus expression-less form.

Finally, to take a numerical order as the main principle of vertical composition is entirely inappropriate, for there is a *qualitative* aspect here: the modeling of the load-bearing [*widerstrebenden*] material from bottom to top. With symmetry the parts were qualitatively the same. Here, the lower parts are the heavy and compressed; the upper, the light and more finely fashioned. Numerical ratios, such as the Golden Section (over-valued by Zeising), come in here as somewhat secondary, but above all we demand to see this qualitative progression expressed from bottom to top.

The laws of this progression defy mathematical definition. A rusticated ground floor of the same height as the second floor above it with a *smooth* wall does not function as 1:1, for with dissimilar materials the visual surfaces no longer decide the matter.

Here too the principle is borrowed from organic structures. We find this evolution from the raw to the refined most completely in human beings. Wundt (*Phys. Psych.* II, 186) notes that a repetition of homologous parts takes place, "in the arms and hands the legs and feet are repeated in finer and more complete form. Similarly, the chest repeats the form of the stomach. But where all the other parts are repeated just twice in the vertical structuring of the form, on top of the trunk we find the head, so that the whole terminates in the most developed part, and the only one that is not homologous to any other". In this principle of vertical development, architecture has a rich opportunity to express character, but this does not come from proportion, nor formal quality, but from internal determinants. For that reason more about this not until later.

The final aspect of Form and the one that is the most mysterious is harmony, "the vital dynamic unity of a clearly differentiated multiplicity". "It arises out of the unity of the inner Life Force. It brings unity to the parts, because it is the parts" (Vischer).

Harmony is a concept best defined, in morphology, as an organism.

The individual is a unitary collective in which all the parts work together toward the same purpose (unity). This purpose is an inner one (self-determination). And the inner purpose is at the same time also an outer dimension, but one beyond which the evolution of vitality (*die Entwicklung des Lebendigen*) does not extend. (Form = inner purpose.)

These statements come from Virchow. They can be assimilated directly into aesthetics.

Kant incidentally, had already said the same, in another context. Under the title, "Architecture of Pure Reason", he gives an outstanding elaboration of what we call Organism and Harmony. He calls it System. The definitions of this are so felicitous that I want to set down their main points.

By System is to be understand the unity of manifold parts within one idea. This idea contains the purpose and form of the Whole, which is congruent with the System (that is Form = inner purpose). The unity of purpose ensures that no part will be lacking, and that no random additions can be made. The whole is therefore articulated and not just heaped together. It can to be sure grow internally, but not externally, like an *animal's body* whose growth adds no limb but, without changing the proportions, makes each one stronger and more capable in its purpose.

With this, everything has been said that could reasonably be said, and it is very significant that architecture has provided the term for this concept.

In harmony there is no expression. It indicates only that which others have called by another name, the *purity* of Form. Purity consists of this, that it was not brought about by chance, one this way, one another, but that it appears as the outcome of a basic unity that proves its necessity.

The impression of organicity is above all based, as August *Thiersch* has shown in his highly instructive essay on "Proportion", (*Handbuch der Architektur*, published by Durm, etc., Darmstadt, IV. 1) on the repetition of the same proportion in the whole and in the parts.[13] It is the same law that Nature follows in her creations.[14]

With this, we have now gone over the main laws of Form.

We will now examine the actual expressive elements more closely, dealing with them as follows, one after the other

1. The relationship of height to width
2. Horizontal development
3. Vertical development
4. Ornament

4. Characteristics of Proportions

"The decisive factor in architecture is the mass (*die Maase*), the relationships of height and width" (Hermann Grimm).

---

[13] [An English translation of this work, *Proportion in Architecture*, is No.2 in the KeepAhead Press Architectural Theory Texts series. – *trans.*]

[14] To approach these matters more closely is impossible here, for the subject absolutely demands explanatory drawings.

They essentially determine the character of a structure.

It therefore seems very important to me to define the expressive value of proportions.

Let us set aside, first of all, what belongs to the intellectual factor: proportions such as 1:1, 1:2, 1:3 are gratifying because they ensure self-determination. The rule, at once evident to us here, excuses us from asking, why is this so, why is it not something else? The Form appears as a necessity. But there cannot be an Expression in it.

No one who recalls what has been said earlier, about the mechanical meaning of all relations to Form, will contradict me when I compare the relationship of height to width, of vertical to horizontal, to the relationship between rest and exertion, and recognize in it the expressive value of proportion. Here too it is the physical factor that is again the characteristic.

What about the much-vaunted ratio of the Golden Section? Is the unchallengeable pleasure that it instills in us to be judged by the intellectual or by the physical principle? We said of the proportions of 1:1, 1:2, 1:3 that their aesthetic meaning lies in the ease with which we recognize these simple numbers, but this obviously does not apply here. The larger side is not a multiple of the smaller side, for height and width are, in the arithmetical sense, irrational. Yet someone might nevertheless think that we can discover the geometric relationship of the smaller side to the larger, and this to their sum. But where is the whole? Is it believable that in looking at a Golden rectangle we add the width to the height and thereby derive the straight line that represents their sum?

The intellectual factor does not seem to be present here.

Another problem with this explanation is that even a trained eye cannot easily recognize the Golden Section as such. With 1:1 or 1:2 imperfections are noticed immedia-tely, here on the other hand judgement is to a certain extent uncertain. Doubts multiply the longer one thinks about them; so much so that I think that this pleasure must be explained by physical conditions, by the relationship of force and gravity.

Let us look at the characteristics of the range of proportions. The square is called squat, heavy, complacent, homely, good-natured, stupid, and so on. Its distinctiveness lies in the equality of height and width, exertion and rest balance each other completely. We cannot say whether the body lies down or stands up. Increasing its width would make it appear at rest, increasing its height would make it appear to be standing. This is apparent in everyday speech. Very consistently, we say: here *lies* the art gallery and here *stands* the tower.

The cube, through its indifference, acquires the character of absolute immobility. It wishes for nothing. Therefore its characteristics: squat, good-natured, stupid, a progression from physical to moral and finally to intellectual qualities.

By taking on height the squat form changes itself and becomes elegant and strong, and finally unstable and elegant, and its form then seems to degenerate into the turmoil of eternal yearning.

By contrast, as the width increases there takes place a development of the proportions from the clumsy and compact to the ever-freer and more relaxed, which however in the end loses itself in debilitating frailty. One gets the impression that without any constraints the figure would have to continue spreading itself out on the flat ground.

(This characteristic, I would note in passing, has been observed in numerous experiments with people of all ages.)

All this suffices to show that the relationship of height and width indicate force and gravity, exertion and rest. These ratios determine expression to an unusually great extent.

What we ourselves know to be comfortable stretching, calm relaxation, we transfer to the distribution of mass, and enjoy the serene calm that buildings of this kind convey. By the same token we also know the state of mind when one "pulls oneself together" in a forceful, serious, posture – and so on.

It seems to me that this is the reason why the Golden Section is favorably positioned in the range of possible combinations, for its striving does not consume itself or push itself upward in breathless haste, but instead knows how to join a powerful will with a calm and secure posture. The horizontal Golden rectangle similarly is far removed from an unstable feebleness and from those clumsy forms that are close to being squares.

Thus the Golden Section, with its juxtaposition of calm Matter and thrusting Force, has an *average measure approximating that of a man.* Indeed, I believe that I have observed that thin people are always restless, and prefer slender proportions, while strong, stocky people choose the opposite. It would have been desirable for Fechner to have considered this in his famous experiments.

The same holds true of the proportions of triangles.

Of great interest is the relationship between proportions and the *rate of breathing*. There is no doubt that very narrow proportions convey the impression of an almost breathless and hasty thrusting upwards. And naturally so: they immediately suggest the idea of tightness which denies us the possibility of breathing deeply with the necessary lateral expansion.[15] Thus Gothic proportions become oppressive: they leave enough room for one to breathe but when one lives in and with these forms we believe that we sense how they press together, thrusting upward, in their self-consuming tension. The *lines* seem to run with accelerating *speed*. As an example of how little the movement of the eyes determines the speed of lines, we can point to the impression of two wavy lines of different wavelengths. Short waves seem swift and nimble to us, long ones by contrast calm and often weary: here, lively, rapid breathing, there, deep and slow. The length of the wave gives the duration, the height of the wave gives the depth of the breathing. Given the importance of the rate of breathing for the expression of moods, this point is a very important aspect of the historical character. One might make the observation that the older a nation becomes, the more rapidly its architecture begins to breathe, it becomes agitated. The lines of the ancient Doric temple run quietly and calmly: everything is broad and slowly-measured. With the Ionic there is already more rapid movement, a search for what is slender and light, and the closer the ancient culture approached its end, the more it demanded a feverishly accelerating movement. Nations who are

---

[15] [HW marginal note:] "Change 'the idea of tightness which denies us the possibility of breathing deeply with the necessary lateral expansion' to 'the idea of tightness, of being pressed together'".

naturally hot-blooded are the most emotional. One thinks of the breathless haste of Arab decorative lines. Unfortunately, I must satisfy myself with hints, a historical psychology, or better yet, a psychological history of art, must be able to track the growing speed of linear movement with great precision, and will find that it is in decoration that pro-gress always appears first.

There are, incidentally, other ways than planar proportions for conjuring up the impression of rapid movement, but I must stay with my theme here.

Proportions are what a nation claims as its distinctly own. Even if the system of decoration is brought in from outside, the national character will always assert itself in the dimensions of height and width. Who can fail to recognize, in Italian Gothic, the national preference for broad, quiet proportions? And conversely, in the North, does not pleasure in heights and towers assert itself again and again? One might almost say that the contrast between southern and northern attitudes toward life is expressed in the contrast between recumbent and standing proportions – there, pleasure in a quiet existence; here, one of restless pressing forward. One could, for example, trace the entire development of world-views by studying the history of the proportions of gables. I do not fear the criticism that these are trivialities. There are indeed some who have arrived at the conclusion that the narrow gothic pointed arches are merely the result of technical developments, and people who see more in them than that are treated as laughable dilettantes. But if one looks at the overall context one sees those slender people as we encounter them in the paintings of the time; how everything there is stretched out, how movement is graceful and rigid, how each finger is splayed out. No wonder then that architecture also reaches sharply and taperingly up to the heights, and forgets the dignified calm that uniquely characterizes Romanesque buildings. The relationship between bodily structure and the preferred proportions is very clear here. But whether the physical history of the human body determines architectural forms or is determined by them is a question that would lead us further afield than we intend to go here.

In the course of the preceding discussion we may perhaps already have cast doubt on the question of whether can speak of *one* principal proportion, for every building shows an abundance of different proportions. To silence these doubts I would like to introduce, as an experiment, the concept of a *mean proportion*. Everyone must agree that it is possible to speak of all-encompassing proportions in Gothic architecture, but the concept must also be validated for every other style. Comparable to the "median tone" in music, it denotes the normal, natural extent in relation to which the other proportions are modulated, and, in relation to this norm, are experienced as a contraction or an expansion. A combination of influences therefore is present: varying proportions are not thought of in their own right but as complementary parts of an integrated whole. History shows that these combinations proliferate as the art matures. Early art offers little if anything more than simple, autonomous proportions.[16]

---

[16] A discussion of the laws that determine these modulations does not belong here; rather, let me refer back to what was said about the harmony of all-encompassing relationships.

5. Characteristics of Horizontal Structuring

The principle of horizontal structuring is called symmetry. Symmetry however is only the requirement that the parts that lie on either side of a dissimilar center must be the same as each other. There is no expression in it at all, as I have already said above, and what is important is that its center stands out as dominant and thereby establishes the parts on either side of it as dependent. As the history of architectural form is related in principle to the development of organic creations, it is permissible to point out here a principle of morphology: "The subordination of parts indicates a more perfected creature. The more that the parts resemble each other, the less are they subordinated to each other." Progress in development is therefore a differentiation (*Gliederung*) of the mass, which always seeks to preserve its consolidated wholeness.

Architectural Form therefore has similarities to human organization and acquires the ability to express everything that is capable of being said by the relationship of the limbs to the body of the human being. Character here lies in the greater or lesser autonomy of these parts. The feeling of freedom stems first and foremost from development of the limbs, which emerge from the body's mass into a life of their own, and the freer the connection to the center, the happier the effect. We find here again that feeling of relaxation and lightness that every cheerful mood arouses. "So free, so relaxed", Vischer once exclaimed.

Tightly-attached lateral parts, on the other hand, lacking independent strength, convey a sense of absolute dependence and complete subordination to the will of the center, just as a person's energetic will is manifested in limbs held closely up against the body.

The implementation of the aforementioned principle is a simple matter, and so I do not need to enumerate all the possible instances of it. The principle is understandable to us on the basis of our own physical organization and our expressive movements, in the application of which architecture is of course not bound to the human analogy; they are combined in a purely schematic way.

We adopt symmetric structuring, or the odd-number division (3-part, 5-part) for everything that stands by itself; for the prominent center, not resembling the parts, represents the inner coherence that is analogous to the construction of our own organization and that of every animal.

We have a decided aversion to bifurcated forms. It is inorganic to let something fall apart in the center.

Bifurcation, however, has been applied with fine sensitivity to dependent forms. In the Greek temple, for example, the front side is symmetrically divided into an odd number of parts; we have five or seven intercolumniations (and it is on these that symmetry depends, and not on the columns, for two columns together are independent, like the two legs of the human body.) On the sides, by contrast, we find an even number of them (intercolumniations), which is to say that the side is not independent by itself, for it has no center, for the center is, rather, taken up by a weight-bearing member.

We find the same thing in other ways as well in the history of architecture. The builder of the Villa Farnesina, for example, created the façade's wings in two segments only, and thereby delicately implied their dependence on the central structure with its five segments.

It is only where it is applied discretely that asymmetry appears as a displacement of balance. Where it is more obvious, it obliges us to take note of each part individually and to regard the whole more as a fortuitous collection than as an organic amalgam.

Nowadays we demand absolute symmetry in monumental buildings: a grave and measured bearing. The Germans of the Middle Ages and of the Renaissance, too, seem to have thought otherwise. They reckoned that each part should function for itself in its own location and seem not to have paid attention to the overall structure, which because of its disunity usually makes a lively rather than a worthy or serious impression on us. We tolerate such freedom only in private or rural buildings.

An idiosyncratic need draws our times toward asymmetry in interior and decorative arts. The restfulness and simplicity of stable equilibrium have become boring; we emphatically seek movement and agitation, in short, the condition of disequilibrium; people no longer want pleasure, as Jacob Burckhardt once said, "but relaxation or distraction, and so the most formless or the most colorful are welcomed". Anyone who wishes to can look for examples of this principle in modern living rooms, where they will find them in abundance.

The modern taste for tall mountains, for the most powerful masses without rule and law, can also be traced back in part to a similar requirement.

But similarly, it is known that a serious injury to the equilibrium can have a depressing effect. We ourselves experience the distressing state of fear and dread when the restfulness of equilibrium cannot be found. I am reminded here of an engraving of Duerer, *Melencolia I.* We see in it a woman in a depressed mood staring at a block of stone. What does it mean? The block of stone is irregular and irrational, it cannot be circumscribed by compass or calipers. But more. When one looks at this stone does it not appear to be falling? Certainly! And the longer one looks at it the more we are drawn into this restlessness. A cube with its absolute equilibrium might be boring but it is satisfied and satisfying; here, on the other hand, we are confronted by the anxious tension of that which cannot achieve a stable form.

The posture of the body conditions the circulation of the blood and the rhythm of breathing. Our observation of the conditions of equilibrium thus leads us to what in architecture is called a *regular sequence* or Eurhythmy (Semper).

We have, in discussing proportion, already dealt with the importance of regularity, as well as of tempo, for all living things.

That a certain measure *irregularity* is allowed within the limits of what has already been formed can be seen by the analogy with symmetry and their common source, the breathing human figure, that is symmetric in its construction and regular in its functions. The same rules apply to both. By easing the law, the highly regular norm can acquire a character that is joyful and free but, beyond that, also one that is dissatisfied and restless. For monumental buildings we unequivocally demand the rule of uniformity; by contrast, a touch of irregularity will heighten the cheerfulness of rural buildings, but it must be very slight for we regard regularity in the same way we do time in music, which may be expanded a little here and there but on the whole must be considered as an inviolable fundamental law.

It seems audacious to speak of the *rhythm* of a sequence, but in view of the fact that we have already referred to a *sequence* of different parts and with it the element of time, why should there not be a rhythm that is based on a stronger emphasis on every second or third part? An example: the Michaelskirche in Hildesheim, where there is a pier after every two pillars.Yet this kind of rhythm is an unusual one, for we also expect a stronger member to carry a greater load, which is not the case here. There remains however yet another possibility, for we can have several varying sequences of elements *next to* and *above* one another, with the weaker elements arranged between the stronger ones, rather like light accompanying figures in music are fitted into the slower, forward-moving main theme. A rhythm that arises in this way is indeed a moment of basic significance, and it plays a not unimportant role in the overall impression.

Let us consider Greek temple architecture:The columns are all like one another, so are the triglyphs that lie above them; what determines the rhythm is whether it is every second or every third triglyphs that is atop a column, in other words, whether the space between two columns is divided into two or three parts. The triglyph recess that corresponds to a column will intuitively seem to be the most strongly emphasized.

In each case the effect is completely different. Where a triglyph is set at the mid-point of an entablature or in the exact center of an intercolumniation, the result for us is an effect of tighter restraint. By contrast, where this point remains unidentified, the effect of this freer arrangement is light and cheerful. Now, this is admittedly not a complete explanation. One would perhaps do well to recall the meaning of 4/4 and 3/4 time for our movement: we march more lightly in 3/4 time. The stressed beat does not always fall on the same foot, but changes; the pace becomes light and airy.[17]

I will refrain from citing further instances. In general, it can be said that only ancient and rigorous art is bifurcated. It was only later on that Graeco-Roman architecture adopted the stimulant – if I may call it that – of 3/4 time. I find it first in the circular temple at Tivoli.

The greatest freedom from restraint manifests itself in rhythms of different series that no longer harmonize together, as in many Renaissance buildings, for example theTempietto of San Pietro in Montorio (Rome)[18] or the vestibule of Santa Maria (Arezzo), etc.

6. Characteristics of Vertical Structuring

We have identified the increasing elaboration of material as the principle of vertical construction. In human beings this elaboration is found in the development of organs that are more refined, that can move more independently of the body and are also themselves articulated in manifold ways. One can compare them in this regard to legs and arms. Our eyes, for example, present us with a similar breaking-through of a closed mass.

What is their equivalent in architecture? It

---

[17] But it is worth considering whether we should give up the idea of the sequence and bring in by way of explanation what we have said above about two- and three-part divisions. It is impossible for me to make up my mind, for many observations and experiments have led to no definite conclusion.

[18] [HW marginal note:] Delete "Tempietto of San Pietro in Montorio (Rome)".

articulates its material in a similar manner and breaks through the wall with openings. As these openings become larger the articulations become more refined and the organs more autonomous. The supporting members that at first appear as wall piers can become free-standing columns with their own sockels. I do not want to enter into details, but rather to state the principle: the unfolding of the vertically acting force of Form.

This force presents itself to us as the same in columns and windows and in cornices. It is invariably a thrusting upward that gravity opposes and usually culminates in a conical form. Below, we find everything is massive, unarticulated, unbroken: this is the base, the sockel; the full force of gravity culminates here. A rusticated ground floor allows for only very small window openings but even then does not seem to preclude the danger that the mass will swallow them up and devour them. That is very understandable to us, and does not offend our feelings.

If however the windows above are missing, Matter persists in its unarticulated wholeness, so that its nature seems to us as if blind, as if trapped in an existence of dullness.[19]

Here architecture approaches human organization in a very notable way, so that physiognomic analogies present themselves in a highly plausible manner.

---

[19] Professor von Brunn calls my attention to a seeming counter-example: the Doge's palace in Venice, while at the same time noting that this exception proves the rule. Here, admittedly, we have above the corridors of the lower floors a massive upper wall with only few windows, albeit this upper wall is beautifully patterned, that is, divided up by form-elements and therefore does not seem heavy; but further – and this is still more notable – it is not topped off by a cornice but dissolves itself in a lacy ornament.

We are used to finding the freest expression where mechanical pressure on a part is eased. This is most clearly expressed in the tails of animals, and among human beings in the head. In architecture, which also has an upward thrust and looks straight ahead (and not onto the ground, like the animal or upward like the plant) the most expressive parts are also the upper ones.

It is to them that our gaze automatically turns, and in them that we find the qualities that define the rest of the building.

The faintest stimulus satisfies our imagination, it settles on single details and requires no additional analogy elsewhere in the structure. Slight though the resemblance of a house is to a human form we nevertheless regard windows as organs that resemble our eyes. One says that they "animate" (*vergeistigen*) a building, and they thereby acquire all the expressive value that lies in the relation of the eye to its surrounding. The part above the window becomes a brow. Joviality must have a smooth brow. Rustication in this area has a very somber effect, particularly if the space is not tall. Thus we cannot escape the impression that the Finance Ministry in Munich has a brow that is frowning, while by contrast a Palazzo Strozzi, with its taller upper wall, does not seem displeased, despite its rustication, but merely serious and consequential. If the windows appear to be directly shaded by a projecting cornice we get an impression of brows that are puckered and pulled down protectively, so to speak, over the eyes.

It would be a not-unthankful task to list the physiognomic possibilities that architecture can embody. It is the *principle,* of course, that is important, and there is certainly no intention to imitate the features of the *human* face. Perhaps, too, the idea of an architectural physiognomy would lose its strangeness in some measure if one were to bear in mind that expressive movements in the human facial muscles are always similar to those of the entire body; so that we raise our eyebrows at the same time as our shoulders; a vertical wrinkling of the brow occurs with a stiffening of the whole body; when a person lowers his brows over his eyes, his head also sinks against his chest. This sufficiently explains the relevance of this principle for non-human subjects.

So much, in short, for this topic, which will become still clearer in the following section.

Before we pass on to ornament, however, another aspect of the character of the vertical Force must briefly be pointed out. Form is action. Every window must at every moment hold its own against the pressure of the material.

Different periods have understood this relationship in different ways.

The round arch is usually regarded as more cheerful than the pointed arch. The one enjoys life – satisfied with its roundness. The other is in its every line exertion and Will; never at ease, it seems to want to force the wall up ever higher.

Striving to express concentrated Will in every form, Gothic architecture has an aversion to all Matter that is dull and clumsy. Anything sluggish or ungrounded is intolerable to it. What she is unable to infuse completely with her Will must vanish. Thus a complete breaking-up of all mass is brought about; the horizontal yields; and the irresistible upward Force, now entirely liberated from gravity, thrusts itself high into the air.

To deconstruct an entire building into its functional components means to want to feel every muscle in one's body. This is the essential meaning of the Gothic. I will return to this again later. Whenever this Force manifests itself in history it is an indication of great perturbance.

The serene calm of the classical age knows nothing like this. In Greek architecture Matter is allowed great scope, the entablature bears down with considerable weight, and it is in the slight rise of the pediment that a modest surplus of vertical Force is apparent. The Greek did not seek to cast off Matter; he enjoyed Force discovering resistance to itself, without seeing in it an obstacle or demanding an unhindered, pointless, reaching for the heights.

It is typical of the modern spirit to prefer that architectural Form work its way laboriously out of Mater. It does not wish to see that which is finished so much as that which is becoming, the unhurried victory of Form.

Renaissance rustication expressed this thought clearly. The Baroque style took the motif further to such an extreme that Form had to work its way out of raw rock.

Antiquity presents perfection as pure and whole and as if it could not be anything else.

As an example, drawn from the realm of theory, of the profound difference between classical and modern outlooks, one could juxtapose the famous statements of Lessing, "Lass mich irren nur lass mich forschen" ("Let me inquire, even if I err") and of Aristotle, *Nic.Eth.*1177 a 26): "εὔλογον δέ τοίς εἰδόσι των ζητούντων ἡδίω τήν διαγωγήν εἶναι" ("Those who know will spend their time more pleasantly than those who inquire").

7. Ornament

Postponing the discussion of ornament until now has been difficult, for it contributes very greatly to the character of horizontal development and even more so to that of vertical development. Yet it seemed to me that the topic should be treated as an integrated whole.

What is ornament? The answer to this question has been obscured in many ways, leading people, like Bötticher in his *Tektonik der Hellenen*, to ask about the canonical meaning of each part, as they believed that they had to search for a closed system, or as they struggled with the question of the historical evolution of a form.

I am in a more fortunate position in that I only want to know one thing: how does ornament *function*?

Wagner (*Handbuch der Arch.*, IV.1, 31*ff.*) distinguishes in the conventional way between decorative and structural ("*konstruktives*") ornament, but has nothing further to say about the decorative than that it "should in a rational way give life to dead surfaces and rigid arrangements"; while he gives to the structural the task of "enhancing and adorning the stylistically-determined art form of the structural components".

Not much can be done with this explanation.

Indeed, the distinction between decorative and structural is of doubtful value. In applying it one immediately bumps up against the consideration that the boundary between the two is a fluid one. In any case, there is little to recommend it as a point of departure, and so I take ornament as a whole and offer the following proposition, which I will validate later, that *Ornament is an expression of abundant force of Form Force (Formkraft)*. The heavy mass puts forth no blossoms.

Let us initially test the value of this definition on a Doric temple.

The entire lower half, from the capital down, shows no decorative forms: neither the temple steps nor the column shaft carry any decorations. In the former we have the raw mass lying heavily there, hardly attaining even the simplest form, while in the latter, the column shaft, we expect the exertion and the concentrated strength that the flutes clearly express; a sculpted column would completely lose the quality of bracing itself up. We will speak about the column in due course. What comes above the columns? The entablature, the load to be carried, a powerful horizontal form. Were the load greater, the columns would give way in the center and the horizontal would be dominant. But conversely, the vertical force is more powerful. It penetrates the weight only faintly to begin with, the architrave remains an unbroken whole, and it is only in the guttae above the column that the effect of the thrust is manifest. Then, after overpowering this initial resistance, the load becomes lighter, and the force breaks through. Vertical elements appear in the triglyphs that extend the fluting motif of the columns, and the metopes that are placed between them express a tectonically independent life, creating space for the unfolding of the finest images, and when at length the mutules fill in the entire span of the entablature they give the impression that the thrust of the columns is gently fading away after having extended itself across the entire entablature. Then follows the supreme achievement: gravity is overcome, the excess of upward force is manifested in the *lifting*[20] of the pediment and celebrates its greatest triumph in plastic figures that, relieved of pressure, are here able to develop themselves freely.[21]

However, even if one concedes what has been said, one finds a contradiction in the capital in the sense that one could say that what appears there is not an excess of Force but, on the contrary, a compression of the column. But that is incorrect. Boettiger found that idea clearly presented in the painted garland of leaves that seemed bowed under by the pressure, but in opposition to that I would like to assert the value of my immediate impression. The leaves give no indication of being pressed down, they bud peacefully out from the echinus. Indeed, what kind of an achievement would it be if the entire weight of the entablature could only bend a few leaves? The motif would be ridiculously petty. In short, it seems to me that the leaves have nothing to do with the conflict between those powerful masses, but are only possible because the free life of the column has not been killed off by the load.

---

[20] Vischer once asked whether the gable rises or falls. Both. It is lifted up in the center, the expression of which is in the ridge tiles; and the flanking lines flow downward, for in the (sideward-facing) *akroteria* the developing force is deflected back. (The steeper the gable, the more evident must these *akroteria* be.) The Gothic, by contrast, displays excessive vertical force in the *crockets.*

[21] A correspondence between the figures on a pediment and the number of triglyphs possibly suggests itself. This is not something I have examined, but I do notice, for example in the Temple of Aegina, a correspondence of this type: eleven triglyphs, 11 figures. On the striking connection between architecture and composition in the Gigantomachy in Pergamon, comp. Brunn's essay (Berlin 1885), p. 50.

It is important to be clear that compression can never be effective aesthetically. Autonomy (*Selbstbestimmung*) is the first commandment. Every form must be justified in itself. And that is also the case here. The column spreads itself out on top because it is functional for it to take the load broadly, and not because it is being squashed.[22] It still has sufficient strength to contract again (directly under the abacus). And it is precisely in the extent to which the mass spreads itself out that the guarantee of its autonomy lies. It goes as far as the abacus reaches. But the abacus – and here one can marvel at the architectural refinement of feeling of the Greeks – this abacus reflects the proportions of the entire entablature. That is to say, the column knows exactly what it must support and acts accordingly.

In Ionic architecture, as we have already observed, an ambition to move more freely is present, a desire not to carry such a heavy load any longer. The pressure on the column is eased and the impression of greater lightness is achieved mainly by letting the excessive force be shed into the volutes (which does not happen in the unpainted Doric columns). In comparative assessments of Doric and Ionic columns I have often had occasion to hear it said that the Ionic holds its head high and the Ionic bends it down. The ancients themselves seem to have had this impression, at least if one may point to the telamones of Akragas and the caryatids of the Erechtheion as Doric and Ionic, respectively. I believe that that is justified. Indeed, it has even happened to me that someone who has not seen either the telamones nor the caryatids has characterized Doric columns with their

---

[22] Naturally, this is not to deny that there can be some elastic yielding.

echinus as very similar to someone spreading out their elbows and bending his head, and by the same token to describe the volutes of the Ionic column as the freefalling hair of a completely upright figure.

We can illustrate the relationship between the two styles with the pointed remark of Goethe (in his essay on architecture written in 1788), "it is human nature always to press further on, even beyond one's goal, and so it is also natural that in the relationship of a column's thickness to its height the eye continuously seeks for more slender proportions and that the mind believes that it senses *greater grandeur and freedom.*"

More grandeur and freedom! That is the urge that led from the Romanesque style to Gothic forms. In these prolegomena, which are always only no more than suggestive, I cannot enter into an analysis of those decorations. But on the basis of the principles given previously that would not be difficult to do. One can readily recognize that all the fireworks of Gothic ornament are possible only because the enormous excess of Form Force over Matter. Ornament is the blossoming of a force that needs accomplish nothing further. It was a very valid feeling that morphed the capital into a light garland of leafy decoration, for the Gothic pillar thrust upward without any diminution of its strength. The Italian Renaissance later on was similarly sensitive when it would not allow an arch to be placed directly above a capital but inserted an entablature between them, so that the column might break itself on it rather in the way that a current of water breaks itself on a barrier. It is an indication of the deep architectural insight of Brunellesco that he recognized the need for this, but it also confirms that our thesis was not simply plucked out of the air but is valid in its essential points.

That is why I may be allowed to hope that no further analysis will be expected here, and I will conclude this section[23] with a historical observation.

Mature cultures always require a great excess of Form Force ("*Formkraft*") over Matter. The calming effect of compact masses of masonry becomes unbearable. One demands movement and excitement, as we have already had the opportunity to note. In the context of decoration the result is an art whose sensibilities nowhere allows calm surfaces but demands throbbing life in every muscle. Thus in the Gothic, in the Arabian and – under very different architectural conditions – the same symptoms in later Rome, too. People "animate" ("*beleben*") every surface with niches, pilasters, etc., only in order to express the agitation they feel coursing through their own bodies and that will no longer allow them to find any pleasure in a calm existence.

8. Principles of Historical Judgement

We have seen thus far how the general condition of the human being establishes what is normative in archi-

---

[23] A secondary source of architectural ornament are the "suspended" decorations, i.e., rings, hangings, bands and such. These should not really be called architectural for they are a carrying over of the manner in which the *completed human* form is adorned. They work in very much the same way as here, namely conveyed by tactile sensation. Cinctured columns, for example, arouse the same feelings as a bare arm that is encircled by a band. After the masterly development of the principles of ornament that Lotze gave in his *Mikrokosmos* (II: 203, ff) there is no need for me to say anything further about this.

tecture. This principle may be taken further: an architectural style mirrors *the bearing and movement* of people of its period. How they carry themselves and move is expressed first and foremost in their clothing, and it is not difficult to show that a period's architecture corresponds with its costumes. I want to emphasize this principle of historical characterization all the more forcefully because I am unable to explore it thoroughly here.

The Gothic style can serve as an example.

Luebke recognized it as the expression of spiritualism. *Semper* called it lapidary scholasticism. What is the principle by which it has been judged? The *tertium comparationis* is not all that clear, for all that there may some validity in each of these descriptions. We can be at a secure starting point only by applying these psychological things to the human figure.

The intellectual fact here is the urge to be precise, sharp and conscious of the will. Scholasticism manifests very clearly the rejection of anything that is imprecise; its concepts are worked out with the highest degree of precision.

In physical terms, this ambition presents itself in the most precise movement, with all forms pointed, no indulgences, nothing vague, and all in all a most clearly expressed will.

Scholasticism and spiritualism can be regarded as the expression of the Gothic only if one keeps in sight this middle stage in which the psychological is directly transposed into bodily form. The pedantic subtlety of the scholastic centuries, and the spiritualism that tolerated no Matter stripped of Will, can only have shaped architectural form through their bodily expression.

Here we find the Gothic forms presented in principle: the bridge of the nose becomes narrower, the forehead sets itself into perpendicular, hard, folds, the entire body stiffens, pulls itself together, as calm broadness disappears. It is well known that many people (particularly, academics) sharpen their thoughts by rolling a well-sharpened pencil back and forth between their fingers and in this way strengthen their thinking. A round pencil would be unable to perform this function. What does roundness want? No one knows. And so too with the Romanesque rounded arch: no definite Will can be discovered in it. It climbs upward, to be sure, but this urge to ascend first finds clear expression in the pointed arch.

The human foot points forward but that is not evident in the blunt line in which it ends. To the Gothic mind it was intolerable that there was no precise expression of a Will here, and so they had their shoes terminate in a pointed beak. (The so-called Cracow shoe appears in the 12th century, cf. Weiss, *Kostümkunde, IV*:8).

The width of the sole is a function of the weight of the body. But the body has no rights, it is Matter, and no concessions may be made to brainless Matter; Will must be able to penetrate every part.

That is why architects dissolved the wall into vertical sections, and the human sole becomes a shoe with three tall heels, as a result of which the impression of a broad sole is disposed of.

I will not pursue here the question of how the principle of the gable shows itself in pointed hats, how all these movements are so stiff, graceful and also so lively and precise, how (as I have already noted) the bodies themselves appear to be stretched out and to have become too thin[24] - I am satisfied if my meaning is now clear.

Traveling through history, one notices with amazement how architecture everywhere imitates the human ideal of bodily form and bodily movement, and how great *painters* have created appropriate architecture for their figures. Do not the buildings of a Rubens pulsate with the same life that streams through his bodies?

I conclude here. It was not my intention to present a complete psychology of architecture, but I very much hoped to make clear the idea that an organic understanding of the history of Forms can become possible when we know which the threads are that bind our Form Imagination (*"Formphantasie"*) to human nature.

A historian evaluating a style has no organon of characteristics, but can only be directed by intuitive guesswork.

The ideal of "working exactly" is also inherent in the historical disciplines. Art historians pursue it, above all, in order to avoid the baleful contact with aesthetics; and often exert themselves merely to say what happened after what – and nothing more than that. Although I am not inclined to underestimate its positive aspects, I must nevertheless believe that the highest goals of scholarship are not to be reached in this way. A history that always limits itself only to the sequence of events in time cannot survive; it would deceive itself, in particular, if it believed itself to have become, in this way, "exact". One can work with exactitude only where it is possible to capture the flow of phenomena in fixed forms. Mechanics, for

---

[24] One must of course not forget that paintings, and even more so statues, are not reliable sources here.

instance, provides physics with such fixed forms. The humanities are still without this foundation; it can only be sought in psychology. This would make it possible for art history to trace the individual phenomenon back to general phenomena and to laws. Psychology to be sure is far removed from a state of perfection in which it could present itself as an organon of historical characteristics, but I do not regard that as an unattainable goal.

One could object that a psychology of art that traces the origins of the impressions we receive back to the Forms and proportions engendered by national feeling (*Volksgefühl*), rests on conclusions that are unjustified, for proportions and lines do not always mean the same thing, and the human sense of Form (*Formgefühl*) is changeable.

This objection cannot be refuted as long as we have no psychological foundation; but as soon as the organization of the human body is shown to be the constant thread in all change, we are defended from this charge, for the uniformity (*Gleichförmigkeit*) of this organization also guarantees the uniformity of the sense of Form.

Furthermore, that styles are not created at the whim of individuals but grow out of national feeling (*Volksgefühl*); and that the individual can only create successfully by submerging himself in the universal, and by perfectly representing the character of the nation and of the age, is too universally known to require further discussion. But even if the sense of Form (*Formgefühl*) remains qualitatively unchanged, one should not fail to recognize fluctuations in its intensity.There have been few periods in which every Form has been purely understood, that is, experienced, and they are the only ones that have created their own styles.

However, because the large architectural forms cannot accommodate itself to every small shift in the national temper *(Volksgemüts)* a gradual estrangement occurs, and the style becomes a lifeless thing that continues to maintain itself only by tradition. The individual forms are used but not understood, and are applied inappropriately, and thus utterly deadened.

The pulse of the age must be sought elsewhere: in the minor decorative arts, in the lines of ornament, in lettering, and so on.[25] *Here the sense of Form satisfies itself in the purest manner, and here too must one search for the birthplace of a new style.* This is a fact of great importance for refuting the materialistic fallacy that seeks to explain the history of architectural Form on the basis of the simple requirements of materials, climate and function. I am far from minimizing the significance of these factors, but must insist that a people's authentic Form-Imagination can never be deflected into other directions by them. What a nation has to say it always will say, and if we observe its language of Form *(Formensprache)* where it speaks without constraint, and if we then find the same Forms, the same lines, the same proportions in its great art of architecture, then we may surely demand that those mechanical observations be silenced.

And with that the most dangerous opponent of the psychology of art will have left the field.

---

[25] Since we began to print from cast-metal fonts this easy flexibility has disappeared. We have nowadays become accustomed (in standard German type) to place Baroque uppercase letters in front of Gothic lowercase ones. See Bechstein, *Die deutsche Druckshrift,* 1865.

German Text

Vorrede

Den Gegenstand der vorliegenden Betrachtungen bildet die Frage, die mir immer als eine überaus merkwürdige erschien: Wie ist es möglich, dass architektonische Formen Ausdruck eines Seelischen, einer Stimmung sein können?

Ueber die Thatsache darf kein Zweifel sein. Nicht nur bestätigt das Urteil des Laien aufs entschiedenste, dass jedes Gebäude einen bestimmten Eindruck mache, vom Ernsten, Düstern bis zum Fröhlich-Freundlichen - eine ganze Skala von Stimmungen, sondern auch der Kunsthistoriker trägt kein Bedenken aus ihrer Architektur Zeiten und Völker zu charakterisieren. Die Ausdrucksfähigkeit wird also zugegeben. Aber wie? Nach welchen Prinzipien urteilt der Historiker?

Ich wunderte mich, dass die wissenschaftliche Litteratur für solche Fragen fast gar keine Antwort hatte. Soviel Sorgfalt und hingebende Liebe dem analogen Problem in der Musik zugewandt worden ist, die Architektur hat weder von der Psychologie noch von der Kunsttheorie eine ähnliche Pflege je genossen. Ich führe das nicht an, um nun selbst mit dem Anspruch aufzutreten, die Lücke zu füllen, vielmehr möchte ich daraus eine Entschuldigung für mich ableiten.

Mehr als einen *Entwurf* darf man nicht erwarten. Was ich hier gebe, sollen lediglich Prolegomena sein zu einer Psychologie der Architektur, die erst noch beschrieben werden muss. Für die oft bloss andeutende Behandlung des Themas bin ich also genötigt, die Gunst, dieses Titels in Anspruch zu nehmen.

1. Psychologische Grundlage

Die Psychologie der Architektur hat die Aufgabe, die seelischen Wirkungen, welche die Baukunst mit ihren Mitteln hervorzurufen im Stande ist, zu beschreiben und zu erklären.

Wir bezeichnen die Wirkung, die wir empfangen, als *Eindruck*.

Und diesen Eindruck fassen wir als *Ausdruck des Objekts*.

Also dürfen wir das Problem auch so formuliren:

Wie können tektonische Formen Ausdruck sein?

(Unter "tekton. Formen" müssen auch die kleinen Künste der Dekoration und des Kunsthandwerks begriffen werden, da sie unter denselben Bedingungen des Ausdrucks stehen.)

Von zwei Seiten kann man versuchen, eine Antwort auf die Frage zu gewinnen: vom Subjekt aus und vom Objekt aus.

Es ist beides geschehen.

Ich erwähne zuerst die vielverbreitete These, die den Gefühlston von Formen erklärt aus den *Muskelgefühlen des Auges*, das mit dem Punkte des deutlichsten Sehens den Linien nachfolgt. Wellenlinie und Zickzack unterscheiden sich für unser Gefühl sehr wesentlich.

Worin liegt der Unterschied?

Im einen Fall, sagt man, ist die Bewegung für das nachzeichnende Auge leichter als im anderen. - "Wo das Auge sich frei bewegt, da verfolgt es seinem physiologischen Organismus gemäss in vertikaler und horizontaler Richtung genau die gerade Linie, jede schräge Richtung aber legt es in einer Bogenlinie zurück." (Wundt, *Vorlesungen* II. 80.)

Daher das Behagen an der Wellenlinie, die Unlust am Zickzack. Schönheit der Form ist identisch mit Angemessenheit für unser Auge. - Es ist die gleiche Anschauung, wenn man behauptet: der Zweck eines Säulenkapitells sei, das Auge von der Vertikale sachte zur Horizontale überzuführen, oder wenn man die Schönheit einer Berglinie darin erblickt, dass das Auge, ohne zu stolpern, sanft an ihr niedergleiten könne.

Wenn mans so hört, möchts leidlich scheinen. Allein es fehlt der Theorie die Hauptsache: die Bestätigung durch die Erfahrung. Man frage sich doch selbst: Wie viel von dem thatsächlichen Eindruck einer Form kann aus Muskelgefühlen erklärt werden? Darf die grössere oder geringere Leichtigkeit, mit der die Bewegung des Auges ausgeführt wird, als das Wesentliche in der Mannigfaltigkeit der Wirkungen gelten? - Die oberflächlichste psychologische Analyse muss zeigen, wie wenig dadurch das Thatsächliche getroffen ist. Ja, man kann diesem Moment nicht einmal eine sekundäre Stellung einräumen. Schon *Lotze* bemerkt sehr richtig, indem er auf das gleichmässige Gefallen einer Wellenlinie und eines rechtwinkligen Mäanders hinweist, dass wir in unserm ästhetischen Urteil die körperliche Mühe stets abziehen, dass also die Wohlgefälligkeit nicht auf der Bequemlichkeit der

Verrichtungen beruht, durch welche wir uns die Wahrnehmung verschaffen. (*Gesch. der Aesthetik in Deutschland* S. 310 f.)

Der Fehler, der hier offenbar vorliegt, scheint daher zu rühren, dass man, weil das Auge die körperlichen Formen wahrnimmt, die optischen Eigenschaften derselben für das Charakteristische hielt. Das Auge scheint aber nur auf die Intensität des Lichts entschieden mit Lust oder Unlust zu reagiren, für Formen indifferent zu sein, den Ausdruck wenigstens durchaus nicht zu bestimmen.

Wir müssen uns also nach einem anderen Prinzip umsehen. Die Vergleichung mit der Musik soll es uns zeigen. Dort haben wir ja das gleiche Verhältnis. Das Ohr ist das perzipirende Organ, aus der Analyse der Gehörsvorgänge aber könnte der Stimmungsgehalt der Töne niemals begriffen werden. Um die Theorie des musikalischen Ausdrucks zu verstehen, ist es nötig, *die eigene Hervorbringung der Töne*, die Bedeutung und Verwendung *unserer Stimmittel* zu beobachten.

Hätten wir nicht die Fähigkeit, selbst in Tönen Gemütsbewegungen auszudrücken, wir könnten nie und nimmer die Bedeutung fremder Töne verstehen. Man versteht nur, was man selbst kann.

So müssen wir auch hier sagen: *Körperliche Formen können charakteristisch sein nur dadurch, dass wir selbst einen Körper besitzen.* Wären wir bloss optisch auffassende Wesen, so müsste uns eine ästhetische Beurteilung der Körperwelt stets versagt bleiben. Als Menschen aber mit einem Leibe, der uns kennen lehrt, was Schwere, Contraktion, Kraft u. s. w. ist, sammeln wir an uns die Erfahrungen, die uns erst die

Zustände fremder Gestalten mitzuempfinden befähigen. - Warum wundert sich Niemand, dass der Stein zur Erde fällt, warum scheint uns das so ganz natürlich? Wir haben nicht die Spur eines Vernunftgrundes für den Vorgang, in unserer Selbsterfahrung liegt allein die Erklärung. Wir haben Lasten getragen und erfahren, was Druck und Gegendruck ist, wir sind am Boden zusammengesunken, wenn wir der niederziehenden Schwere des eigenen Körpers keine Kraft mehr entgegensetzen konnten, und darum wissen wir das stolze Glück einer Säule zu schätzen und begreifen den Drang alles Stoffes, am Boden formlos sich auszubreiten.

Man kann sagen, das habe keine Beziehung auf die Auffassung *linearer und planimetrischer Verhält-nisse*. Allein diesem Einwurf liegt nur mangelhafte Beobachtung zu Grunde. Sobald man Acht hat, wird man finden, dass wir auch solchen Verhältnissen eine mechanische Bedeutung unterschieben, dass es keine schräge Linie giebt, die wir nicht als ansteigend, kein schiefes Dreieck, das wir nicht als Verletzung des Gleichgewichts empfänden. Dass nun aber gar architektonische Gebilde nicht bloss geometrisch, sondern als *Massenformen* wirken, sollte eigentlich kaum gesagt zu werden brauchen. Dennoch macht eine extrem formalistische Aesthetik immer wieder jene Voraussetzung.

Wir gehen weiter. Die Töne der Musik hätten keinen Sinn, wenn wir sie nicht als Ausdruck irgend eines fühlenden Wesens betrachteten. Dieses Verhältnis, das bei der ursprünglichen Musik, dem Gesang, ein natürliches war, ist durch die Instrumentalmusik verdunkelt, aber durchaus nicht aufgehoben worden. Wir legen den gehörten Tönen immer ein Subjekt unter, dessen Ausdruck sie sind.

Und so in der Körperwelt. Die Formen werden uns bedeutend dadurch allein, dass wir in ihnen den Ausdruck einer fühlenden Seele erkennen. Unwillkürlich beseelen wir jedes Ding. Das ist ein uralter Trieb des Menschen. Er bedingt die mythologische Phantasie und noch heute - gehört nicht eine lange Erziehung dazu des Eindrucks los zu werden, dass eine Figur, deren Gleichgewichtszustand verletzt ist, sich nicht wohl befinden könne? Ja, erstirbt dieser Trieb jemals? Ich glaube nicht. Es wäre der Tod der Kunst. -

Das Bild unserer selbst schieben wir allen Erscheinungen unter. Was wir als die Bedingungen unseres Wohl-befindens kennen, soll jedes Ding auch besitzen. Nicht so, dass wir den Schein eines menschlichen Wesens in den Formen der anorganischen Natur verlangten, aber wir fassen die Körperwelt mit den Kategorien auf (wenn ich so sagen darf), die wir mit derselben gemeinsam haben. Und danach bestimmt sich auch die Ausdrucksfähigkeit dieser fremdartigen Gestalten. *Sie können uns nur das mitteilen, was wir selbst mit ihren Eigenschaften aus*drücken.

Hier wird mancher bedenklich werden und nicht recht wissen, was wir denn für Aehnlichkeiten oder gar welche Ausdrucksorgane wir mit dem toten Stein teilen. Ich will es kurz sagen: es sind die Verhältnisse der Schwere, des Gleichgewichts, der Härte u. s. w., lauter Verhältnisse, die für uns einen Ausdruckswert besitzen. Der ganze menschliche Gehalt natürlich kann nur durch die menschliche Gestalt ausgedrückt werden, die Architektur wird nicht einzelne Affekte, die sich in bestimmten Organen äussern, zum Ausdruck bringen können. Sie soll es auch nicht versuchen. Ihr Gegenstand bleiben die grossen Daseingefühle, die Stimmungen, die einen gleichmässig andauernden Zustand des Körpers voraussetzen. -

Ich könnte hier schon diesen Abschnitt schliessen und höchstens noch darauf hinweisen, wie sich auch in der Sprache an einer Fülle von Beispielen jene unüberwindliche Neigung unserer Phantasie bekundet, alles Körperliche unter der Form belebter Wesen aufzufassen. Man erinnere sich an die architektonische Terminologie. Wo immer ein abgeschlossenes Ganzes sich darstellt, geben wir ihm Kopf und Fuss, suchen nach Vorder- und Hinterseite etc.

Allein es bleibt noch die Frage, wie nun die Beseelung dieser fremden Gestalten zu danken sei. Es ist wenig Aussicht auf eine erfreuliche Lösung. Aber ich will nicht darüber hinweggehen, weil von anderer Seite auch schon dies Ziel ins Auge gefasst worden ist.

Das antropomorphe Auffassen der räumlichen Gefilde ist nichts Unerhörtes. In der neueren Aesthetik ist dieser Akt bekannt unter dem Namen des S y m b o l i s i r e n s. Joh. Volkelt[1]) hat die Geschichte des Symbolbegriffs geschrieben und sich wesentliche Verdienste um die genauere Fassung dessen erworben, was zuerst von *Herder*[2]) und Lotze [3]) angedeutet worden ist.

---

[1] V o l k e l t, Symbolbegriff in der neueren Ästhetik. Jena 1876.
[2] Ausser der "Kalligone" enthält der Aufsatz "Plastik" bedeutsame Äusserungen.
[3] L o t z e, *Geschichte der Ästhetik in Deutschland* a. v. O.- , Microcosmos II[3] 198 ff.

Nach Volkelt vollzieht sich die Symbolisirung räum-licher Gebilde folgendermassen (*Symbolbegr.* 51-70.):

1) Das räumliche Gebilde wird auf Bewegung und auf Wirkung von Kräften gedeutet, ein Akt, der noch nicht eigentlich symbolisch zu nennen ist: mit dem Auge dem Umriss der Erscheinungen nachfolgend, bringen wir die Linien in ein lebendiges Rinnen und Laufen.

2) Um das räumliche Gebilde ästhetisch zu verstehen, müssen wir diese Bewegung sinnlich miterleben, mit unserer körperlichen Organisation mitmachen.

3) Mit der bestimmten Erstreckung und Bewegung unseres Körpers ist ein Wohl und Wehegefühl verbunden, das wir als eigentümlichen Genuss jener Naturgestalten selber auffassen.

4) Um ästhetisch zu heissen, muss aber dieses Wohl und Wehegefühl eine geistige Bedeutung haben, Körpererbewegung und physisches Gefühl müssen Ausdruck einer Stimmung sein.

5) Die Thatsache, dass wir im ästhetischen Geniessen unsere ganze Persönlichkeit beteiligt finden, beweist, dass in jedem Genuss etwas von dem allgemein menschlichen Gehalte, von den Ideen, die das Menschliche konstituiren enthalten sein muss.

So weit die Analyse *Volkelts*..

Im wesentlichen bin ich vollständig einverstanden. Die Bedenken, die etwa gegen den 1. Punkt und gegen die Trennung des 3. und 4. geäussert werden könnten, sollen hier unterdrückt werden. Ich möchte die ganze Aufmerksamkeit richten auf den Kern der Sache, auf den zweiten Satz: das Miterleben der fremden Form. Wie ist das zu denken: "Wir durchdringen mit unserm Körpergefühl das Objekt"? *Volkelt* hält sich hier absichtlich mit seinen Ausdrücken in einer Sphäre der Dunkelheit und findet später (mit F r. *Vischer*) die einzige Lösung in einer pantheistischen Auffassung der Welt. Er will dem geheimnisvollen Prozess nicht zu nahe treten: "Mit meinem Vitalgefühl lege ich mich dunkel in das Objekt hinein" sagt er (pg.61), anderswo spricht er von einer "Selbstversetzung" u. s. f. Zugegeben, dass man den ganzen Verlauf dieses psychischen Aktes nicht bloslegen kann, so möchte ich doch fragen: Ist dies Miterleben ein *sinnliches* oder vollzieht es sich bloss in der *Vorstellung*? Mit andern Worten: Erleben wir die fremden Körperformen an unsrem eignen Leibe?

Oder: ist das Mitfühlen der fremden Zustände etwas, was allein der Thätigkeit der Phantasie angehört?

Volkelt bleibt hier schwankend. Bald sagt er: Wir müssen das Objekt, mit unsrer körperlichen Organisation s i n n l i c h miterleben (pg. 57), bald aber wieder ist es die blosse Phantasie, die die Bewegung ausführt (pg. 61, 62.)

Lotze und Rob. Vischer[41]), die zuerst die Bedeutung des körperlichen Miterlebens geltend gemacht

---

[4] Rob. Vischer, *Das optische Formengefühl*. Leipzig, 1872

haben, dachten offenbar nur an Prozesse, die sich in der Phantasie vollziehen. In diesem Sinn heisst es bei *Rob Vischer*: "Wir besitzen das wunderbare Vermögen unsre eigne Körperform einer objektiven Form zu unterschieben und einzuverleiben." Bei *Lotze* ebenso: "Keine Gestalt ist so spröde, in die hinein unsere P h a n t a s i e sich nicht mitlebend zu versetzen wüsste."

Wenn ich also recht verstehe, ist V o l k e l t hier über seine Vorgänger hinausgeschritten, ohne aber das Problem genauer ins Auge zu fassen.

Ueber die Berechtigung der Frage darf kein Zweifel sein. Denn die körperlichen Affektionen, die wir bei der Betrachtung architektonischer Werke empfangen, sind nicht zu läugnen. Ich könnte mir also wohl denken, dass jemand mit der Behauptung aufträte, der Stimmungseindruck der Architektur beruhe allein darin, dass wir unwillkürlich mit unsrer Organisation die fremden Formen nachzubilden versuchen, mit andren Worten, dass wir die Daseinsgefühle architektonischer Bildungen nach der körperlichen Verfassung beurteilen, in die wir geraten. Kräftige Säulen bewirken in uns energische Innervationen, nach der Weite oder Enge der räumlichen Verhältnisse richtet sich die Respiration, wir innerviren als ob wir diese tragenden Säulen wären und atmen so tief und voll, als wäre unsre Brust so weit wie diese Hallen, Asymmetrie macht sich oft als körperlicher Schmerz geltend, uns ist, als ob uns ein Glied fehlte oder verletzt sei, ebenso kennt man den unleidlichen Zustand, den der Anblick gestörten Gleichgewichts hervorruft u. s. w. Es wird jeder in seiner Erfahrung ähnliche Fälle finden. Und wenn *Goethe* gelegentlich sagt, die Wirkung eines schönen Raumes müsste man haben, wenn man auch mit verbundenen Augen hindurchgeführt würde, so ist das nichts andres als der Ausdruck desselben Gedankens: dass der architektonische Eindruck, weit entfernt etwa ein "Zählen des Auges" zu sein, wesentlich in einem unmittelbaren körperlichen Gefühl beruhe.

Statt einer unbegreiflichen "Selbstversetzung" hätten wir uns dann etwa vorzustellen, der optische Nervenreiz löse direkt eine Erregung der motorischen Nerven ein, die die Kontraktion von bestimmten Muskeln veranlasse. Man könnte als verdeutlichendes Gleichnis die Thatsachen anführen, dass ein Ton den verwandten überall mitklingen macht.

Was könnte der Verteidiger einer solchen Ansicht etwa sagen?

Er würde wohl anknüpfen an menschliche Uebertragung des Ausdrucks, an die neuerdings lebhaft vertretene Theorie, dass das Verständnis menschlichen Ausdruckes sich vermittle durch Nacherleben.

Es liessen sich dabei folgende Sätze formulieren:

1) Jede Stimmung hat ihren bestimmten Ausdruck, der sie regelmässig begleitet; denn Ausdruck ist nicht nur eine Fahne gleichsam, ausgehängt, um zu zeigen, was innen vorgehe, nicht etwas, was ebensogut fehlen könnte, Ausdruck ist vielmehr die körperliche Erscheinung des geistigen Vorgangs. Er besteht nicht bloss in den Spannungen der Gesichtsmuskeln oder den Bewegungen der Extremitäten, sondern erstrekt sich auf den gesamten Organismus.

2) Sobald man den Ausdruck eines Affekts nachbildet, wird sich demnach der Affekt selbst sofort auch einstellen. Unterdrückung des Ausdrucks ist Unterdrückung des Affekts. Umgekehrt wächst dieser je mehr man im Ausdruck ihm nachgiebt. Der Furchtsame wird furchtsamer, wenn er auch in den Geberden seine Unruhe zeigt.

3) Ein unwillkürliches Nachbilden des Ausdrucks fremder Personen und somit eine Uebertragung von Gemütsbewegungen kann oft beobachtet werden. Man weiss, wie Kinder jedem starken Eindruck haltlos preisgegeben sind, sie können z. B. niemanden weinen sehen, ohne selbst die Thränen laufen zu lassen u. s. f. Nur in Zuständen des energisch betonten Selbstgefühls sind sie hiefür unzugänglich, weil dies Nacherleben einen gewissen Grad von Willenlosigkeit voraussetzt. Später bewirkt überdies Erziehung und vernünftiges Ueberlegen, dass man sich nicht jedem Eindruck "hingibt". In gewissen Momenten aber "vergisst man sich" dennoch und macht Bewegungen, die nur Sinn hätten, wenn wir die fremde Person wären.

Solche Fälle von Selbstversetzung sind z. B. folgende:

Es versucht jemand mit heiserer Stimme zu sprechen. Wir räuspern uns. - Warum? Wir glauben in diesem Augenblicke selbst heiser zu sein und wollen nun uns davon befreien (oder wenigstens der Klarheit unsrer Stimme uns versichern).

Weiter geschieht es bei einer schmerzlichen Operation oft, dass wir die Züge des Leidenden genau nachbilden, ja sogar an der betroffenen Stelle selbst einen lebhaften Schmerz empfinden.

Das sind nun aussergewöhnliche Fälle und man darf nicht läugnen, dass sich im flüchtigen Alltagsleben das körperliche Miterleben fast spurlos verloren hat und wir die Ausdrucksformen unsrer Nebenmenschen hinnehmen wie Rechenpfennige, deren Wert wir aus Erfahrung kennen. Immerhin bleibt ein Reiz, wenn auch der eingedrückte Ausdruck - wenn ich so sagen darf - nicht bis zur Oberfläche dringt (also in Gesicht und Haltung sich geltend macht.) Denn die *innern* Organe vor allem werden sympathisch berührt und nach meinen Beobachtungen ist es die *Respirationsbewegung*, die am empfänglichsten ist für Veränderungen. Der Rhythmus des Atmens, den wir bei andren wahrnehmen, überträgt sich am leichtesten auf uns. Einem Erstickenden zuzusehen ist fürchterlich, weil wir die ganze Qual mitempfinden, während wir stumpfer bleiben beim Anblick anderen körperlichen Schmerzes. Diese Thatsache ist wichtig, weil gerade der Atem das unmittelbarste Organ des Ausdruckes ist.

So möchte etwa ein Verteidiger seinen Beweis des körperlichen Miterlebens einleiten, und vielleicht hoffte er auch noch darin eine Stütze zu finden, dass Gesetzmässigkeit empfunden wird, ohne dass der Intellekt sich deren bewusst geworden ist, oder, im umgekehrten Fall, eine Verletzung des Normalen vom

"Auge" oder vom "Gefühl" (wie man sich auszudrücken pflegt) früher empfunden wird, als der Intellekt merkt, wo ein Fehler vorliegt.

Wollte man etwa einwerfen, für die ästhetische Anschauung könne dies Miterleben nicht in Betracht kommen, denn ein Nachbilden des menschlichen, physiognomischen Ausdrucks finde nur statt in *willenlosen* Momenten, wo man *sich vergisst* und ganz sich versenkt in das Objekt, so würde dieser Einwurf zurückgewiesen werden können mit der durchaus richtigen Bemerkung, die ästhetische Anschauung verlange eben diese Willenlosigkeit, dieses Aufgeben des Selbstgefühls. Wer nicht die Fähigkeit hat zeitenweise aufzuhören an sich zu denken, der wird niemals zum Genuss eins Kunstwerks kommen, noch weniger ein solches schaffen können[5].

Dass das *Erhabene* nicht mehr nachgebildet werden kann, müsste auch der Verteidiger dieser These zugeben. Während eine leichte Säulenhalle mit ihrer heitern Kraft uns durchströmt und ein unmittelbares Wohlbehagen hervorruft, stellen sich dort im Gegenteil die Symptome der Furcht ein: Wir fühlen die Unmöglichkeit dem Ungeheuren uns gleichzustellen, die

---

[5] Anm. In diesem psychologischen Tatbestand ist die Verwandschaft des moralischen und des ästhetischen Gemütszustands begründet. Das "Mitleiden", das jener voraussetzt, ist psychologisch der gleiche Prozess, wie das ästhet. Mitfühlen. Daher sind grosse Künstler bekannter Weise immer auch "gute Menschen", d. h. dem Affekt des Mitleids in hohem Grade unterworfen.

Gelenke lösen sich u. s. w. Bei der Sonderstellung des Erhabenen wäre aber das immer noch keine Widerlegung des Hauptsatzes.

Auch das Recht, die Auffassung des menschlichen Ausdrucks überhaupt zu vergleichen mit der Auffassung der architektonischen Formen wird man nicht bestreiten können. Wo sollte die Grenze sein, wo dieses mitfühlende Erleben aufhören? Es wird statthaben, wo immer wir noch gleiche Daseinsverhältnisse mit den unsrigen finden, d. h. wo *Körper* uns entgegentreten.

Weiter verfolgt würde eine derartige Untersuchung zurückführen in die Geheimnisse der psychischen Entwicklungsgeschichte. Und schliesslich, wenn auch ein durchgängiges Erleben konstatiert wäre, wenn wir beweisen könnten, dass unser Körper genau die Veränderungen erleidet, die als Ausdruck der Stimmung, die das Objekt uns mitteilt, entsprechen, was wäre damit gewonnen?

Wer sagt uns, wo die Priorität ist? Ist die körperliche Affektion Bedingung des Stimmungseindrucks? oder sind die sinnlichen Gefühle nur eine Folge der lebhaften Vorstellung in der Phantasie? Oder endlich, die dritte Möglichkeit, gehn Psychisches und Körperliches parallel?

Indem wir die Frage bis zu diesem Punkt getrieben haben, ist es höchste Zeit abzubrechen: denn jetzt stehn wir vor Problemen, die die Grenze aller Wissenschaft bezeich-nen.

Wir ziehen uns zurück. Im Folgenden werden wir keine Rücksicht mehr nehmen auf diese Schwierigkeiten, sondern die herkömmlichen bequemen Ausdrücke auch unsrerseits gebrauchen.

Was als Grundlage gewonnen wurde, ist dieses: *Unsre leibliche Organisation ist die Form, unter der wir alles Körperliche auffassen.* Ich werde nun zeigen, dass die Grundelemente der Architektur: Stoff und Form, Schwere und Kraft sich bestimmen nach den Erfahrungen, die wir an uns gemacht haben; dass die Gesetze der formalen Aesthetik nichts andres sind als die Bedingungen, unter denen uns allein ein organisches Wohlbefinden möglich scheint, dass endlich der Ausdruck, der in der horizontalen und vertikalen Gliederung liegt, nach menschlichen (organischen) Prinzipien gegeben ist.

Dies ist der Inhalt der folgenden Abschnitte.

Es liegt mir nun durchaus fern, zu behaupten, der architektonische Eindruck sei damit vollständig analysiert, gewiss kommen noch sehr viele andere Faktoren hiezu: Farbe, Assoziationen, die aus der Geschichte und Bestimmung des Gebäudes erwachsen, Beschaffenheit des Stoffes etc. Immerhin glaube ich nicht zu irren, wenn ich den Kern des Eindrucks in den hier dargestellten Zügen erblicke.

Es sei gestattet mit Uebergehung der anderen Faktoren hier nur noch andeutend auf das hinzuweisen, was man *Analogien der Linienempfindung* nennen kann.

Unter Analogien der Empfindung versteht nämlich Wundt (*phys. Psych.* I ^{2}, 486 ff.) die Verwandtschaftsverhältnisse, die wir zwischen den Empfindungen disparater Sinne anzunehmen pflegen, wie z. B. zwischen tiefen Tönen und dunkeln Farben, die als reine Empfindungen betrachtet kein Gemeinsames haben, vermöge ihres gleichen ernsten Gefühlstons uns aber verwandt erscheinen.

Solche Analogien stellen sich auch bei Linien ein.Es wäre erwünscht, über diesen ganz unbeachteten Gegenstand einmal etwas Zusammenhängendes zu hören.[6]) Ich gebe einige Bemerkungen, die durch mannigfache Versuche gewonnen worden sind.

Das hastige Auffahren des Zickzacks führt unmittelbar die Erinnerung an brennendes Rot mit sich, während das sanfte Blau einer weichen Wellenlinie sich zugesellt und zwar eine mattere Nüance den langgezogenen Wellen, eine kräftigere den leichter beweglichen. Wie ja auch die Sprache "matt" gleichmässig verwendet für Farbentöne, denen die Leuchtkraft fehlt, und für körperliche Müdigkeit.

Ebenso spricht man von warmen und kalten Linien, von den warmen Linien des Holzschnitts z. B. und den kalten des Stahlstichs, Gegensätze die sich wiederum decken mit den Druckempfindungen: hart und weich.

Am deutlichsten ist die Analogie mit Tönen, wo wahrscheinlich die Erfahrungen an der eigenen Stimme über Tonbildung mitwirken. So beurteilt jedermann eine Linie mit kurzen kleinen Wellen als tremulierend in hoher Lage, weite Schwingungen von geringer Höhe als dumpfhohles Summen. Zickzack "rasselt und klirrt wie Waffenlärm" (Jak. Burkhardt), sehr spitz wirkt er gleich schneidenden Pfeifentönen. Die Gerade ist ganz still.

Es hat also einen guten Sinn auch in der Architektur von der *stillen* Einfalt der Antike und dem widrigen Lärmen z. B. der englischen Gothik zu sprechen; oder etwa in der sanft herabgleitenden Linie eines Berges das leise Verklingen eines Tones zu empfinden.

---

[6] Natürlich müssten hierbei sprachliche Untersuchungen den experimentirenden Psychologen unterstützen.

2. Der Gegenstand der Architektur

Die Materie ist schwer, sie drängt abwärts, will formlos am Boden sich ausbreiten. Wir kennen die Gewalt der Schwere von unserem eigenen Körper. Was hält uns aufrecht, hemmt ein formloses Zusammenfallen? Die gegenwirkende Kraft, die wir als Wille, Leben oder wie immer bezeichnen mögen. Ich nenne sie Formkraft. *Der Gegensatz von Stoff und Formkraft*, der die gesamte organische Welt bewegt, ist das Grundthema der Architektur. Die ästhetische Anschauung überträgt diese intimste Erfahrung unseres Körpers auch auf die leblose Natur. In jedem Ding nehmen wir einen Willen an, der zur Form sich durchzuringen versucht und den Widerstand eines formlosen Stoffes zu überwinden hat.

Mit dieser Erkenntnis haben wir den entscheidenden Schritt gethan, um sowohl die formale Aesthetik durch lebensvollere Sätze zu ergänzen, wie auch um dem architektonischen Eindruck einen reicheren Inhalt zu sichern, als ihm z. B. *Schopenhauers* viel bewunderte Theorie zugestehen will. Glücklicherweise lässt sich niemand den Genuss von der Philosophie trüben und Schopenhauer selbst hatte wohl zu viel Kunstgefühl, um an seinen Satz zu glauben: Schwere und Starrheit seien der einzige Gegenstand der Baukunst. Weil er nicht den Eindruck, die psychische Wirkung der Architektur analysierte, sondern nur ihren Stoff, liess er sich zu dem Schluss verleiten:

1. Die Kunst stellt die Ideen der Natur dar.
2. Der architektonische Stoff bietet als Hauptideen: Schwere und Starrheit.
3. Also ist die Aufgabe der Kunst diese Ideen in ihrem Widerspruch klar darzustellen

Die Last will zu Boden, die Träger, vermöge ihrer Starrheit widersetzen sich diesem Willen.

Abgesehen von der Dürftigkeit dieses Gegensatzes, begreift es sich schwer, wie Schopenhauer verkennen konnte, dass die Starrheit des Steines einer griechischen Säule in der ästhetischen Anschauung vollständig aufgehoben und zu lebendigem Aufstreben verwandelt wird.

Genug, ich wiederhole: Wie die Charakteristik der Schwere unseren körperlichen Erfahrungen entnommen ist, ohne sie unmöglich wäre, so wird auch das, was der Schwere entgegenwirkt, nach menschlicher d. h. organischer Analogie aufgefasst. Und so behaupte ich, dass alle die Bestimmungen, die die formale Aesthetik über die *schöne Form* giebt, nichts anderes sind, als *Bedingungen organischen Lebens.* Formkraft ist also nicht nur als Gegensatz der Schwere, vertikal-wirkende Kraft, sondern das was Leben schafft, eine vis plastica, um diesen in der Naturwissenschaft verpönten Ausdruck hier zu gebrauchen. Ich will im nächsten Abschnitt die einzelnen Formgesetze darlegen. Hier genügt der Hinweis, indem es mir jetzt nur darauf ankommt, den Grundgedanken bestimmt hinzustellen, das Verhältnis von Stoff und Form klar zu legen.

Nach all dem Gesagten kann kein Zweifel sein, dass Form nicht als etwas äusserliches dem Stoff übergeworfen wird, sondern aus dem Stoff herauswirkt, als immanenter Wille; Stoff und Form sind untrennbar. In jedem Stoff lebt ein Wille, der zur Form drängt, aber nur nicht immer sich ausleben kann. Man darf sich auch nicht vorstellen, der Stoff sei das unbedingt feindliche, vielmehr wäre eine stofflose Form gar nicht denkbar;

überall stellt sich das Bild unseres körperlichen Daseins als der Typus dar, nach dem wir jede andere Erscheinung beurteilen. Der Stoff ist das böse Prinzip insofern, als wir ihn als lebensfeindliche Schwere kennen. Zustände der Schwere sind immer verbunden mit einer Verminderung der Lebenskraft. Das Blut läuft langsamer, der Atem wird unregelmässig und seufzend, der Körper hat keinen Halt mehr und sinkt zusammen. Es sind das Momente des Ungleichgewichts, die Schwere scheint uns zu überwältigen. Die Sprache hat dafür den Ausdruck: *Schwermut gedrückte* Stimmung u. s. w. Ich untersuche nicht weiter, welche Störungen physischer Art hier vorliegen: genug, dies ist der Zustand der *Formlosigkeit.*

Alles lebendige sucht sich ihm zu entringen, zur Regelmässigkeit, zum Gleichgewicht zu gelangen, als dem naturgemässen Verhalten. In diesem Versuch des organischen Willens den Körper zu durchdringen, ist das Verhältnis von Form zu Stoff gegeben.

Der Stoff selbst sehnt sich gewissermassen der Form entgegen. Und so kann man diesen Vorgang bezeichnen mit den gleichen Worten, die Aristoteles von dem Verhältnis seiner Formen zum Stoff gebraucht, oder mit einem herrlichen Ausdruck Goethes sagen: das Bild muss sich entwirken. Die vollkommene Form aber stellt sich dar als eine Entelechie, als die Vollendung dessen, was im Stoff angelegt war.

Zu Grunde liegt all diesen Gleichnissen das eine tiefmenschliche Erlebnis von der Formung des Ungeformten. Wenn man die Architektur bezeichnet hat als eine erstarrte Musik, so ist das nur der Ausdruck für die gleiche Wirkung, die wir von beiden Künsten empfangen. Indem hier die rhythmischen Wellen auf uns eindringen, uns ergreifen, uns hineinziehen in die schöne Bewegung, löst sich alles Formlose und wir geniessen das Glück, auf Augenblicke befreit zu sein von der niederziehenden Schwere des Stoffes.

Eine gleiche formende Kraft empfinden wir in jedem architektonischen Gebilde, nur dass sie nicht von aussen kommt, sondern von innen, als gestaltender Wille, ihren Körper sich bildet. Das Ziel ist nicht die Vernichtung des Stoffes, sondern nur die organische Fügung, ein Zustand, von dem wir empfinden, dass er selbstgewollt, nicht durch äussern Zwang entstanden sei; *Selbstbestimmung* ist die Bedingung aller Schönheit. Dass die Schwere des Stoffes überwunden sei, dass in mächtigsten Massen ein unverständlicher Wille sich rein hat befriedigen können, das ist der tiefste Gehalt des architektonischen Eindrucks.

Ausleben der Anlage, Befriedigung des Willens, Befreiung von der stofflichen Schwere - es sagen alle Ausdrücke das gleiche.

Je grösserer Widerstand überwunden ist, desto höher die Lust.

Nun kommt es aber nicht nur darauf an, *dass* ein Wille sich auslebt, sondern *was* für ein Wille. Ein Würfel genügt der ersten Forderung vollkommen, allein es ist ein ausserordentlich dürftiger Inhalt, der hier zu Tage tritt.

Innerhalb der formal korrekten d. h. lebensfähigen Architektur ist eine Entwicklung möglich, die man wohl nicht ganz mit Unrecht mit der Entwicklung der organischen Gebilde vergleichen möchte: es findet der gleiche Fortgang von dumpfen, wenig gegliederten

Gestalten bis zum feinst ausgebildeten System differenzierter Teile statt.

Die Architektur erreicht ihren Höhepunkt jeweilen da, wo aus der ungeteilten Masse einzelne Organe sich losgelöst haben und jedes Glied, seinem Zweck allein nach-kommend, zu funktionieren scheint ohne den ganzen übrigen Körper in Mitleidenschaft zu ziehen oder von ihm behindert zu sein.

Dasselbe Ziel verfolgt die Natur in ihren organischen Gebilden. Die niedrigsten Wesen sind ein Ganzes ohne Gliederung, die notwendigen Funktionen werden entweder von "Scheinorganen" verrichtet, die jeweilen aus der Masse heraustreten und in ihr wieder verschwinden oder es besteht für alle Vorrichtungen nur *ein* Organ, das dann sehr mühsam arbeitet. Die höchsten Wesen dagegen zeigen ein System differenzierter Teile, die unabhängig von einander wirken können. Es bedarf der Uebung, um diese Unabhängigkeit ganz zu entwickeln. Der Rekrut kann anfänglich nicht gehen, ohne den ganzen Körper mit in Anspruch zu nehmen, der Klavierschüler ist nicht im stande einen Finger allein zu heben.

Das Missbehagen solcher Zustände, w o der Wille sich nicht rein zur Geltung bringen kann, wo er gleichsam im Stoff stecken bleibt, ist dasselbe Gefühl, das ungenügend gegliederte Bauwerke uns mitteilen. (Der romanische Stil ist reich an Beispielen der Art).

Deutet so die Selbständigkeit der Teile auf höhere Vollkommenheit des Organismus, so wird uns das Geschöpf noch um so bedeutender, je unähnlicher die Teile einander sind (innerhalb der Schranken natürlich, die durch die allgemeinen Formgesetze gegeben sind, siehe den nächsten Abschnitt.) Die Gothik, die in ihren Teilen immer das gleiche Muster wiederholt: Thurm = F i a l e , Giebel = W i m p e r g, eine unendliche Vielheit gleicher und ähnlicher Glieder gibt, muss hinter der Antike zurückstehen, die nichts wiederholt: *ein*e Säulenordnung, *ein* Gebälk, *ein* Giebel.

Doch ich breche diese Betrachtungen ab. Fruchtbar können sie erst geübt werden, wenn der architektonische Organismus in seinen Teilen schon bekannt ist. Was ich habe zeigen wollen, ist nur das eine, dass wir in unmittelbarem Gefühl die Vollkommenheit architect-onischer Gebilde nach demselben Massstab bemessen, wie die der lebenden Geschöpfe.

Wir wenden uns zu den allgemeinen Formgesetzen.

3. Die Form und ihre Momente

Um eine feste Grundlage zu haben, nehme ich die Bestimmungen der Form, wie sie Fr. *Vischer* in der Selbstkritik seiner Aesthetik gibt (*Krit. Gänge* V).

Er unterscheidet 2 äussere und 4 innere Momente. Die ersten sind:

1) Begrenzung im Raum.
2) Mass, entsprechend der Spannkraft unserer Anschauung (für uns hier unwesentlich).

Dass jedes Ding, um Individuum zu sein, gegen seine Umgebung sich abgrenzen muss, ist conditio sine qua non. Ueber die Art der Abgrenzung wird gleich gesprochen werden.

Als innere Momente treten auf:

1) Regelmässigkeit.
2) Symmetrie.
3) Proportion.
4) Harmonie.

Indem ich mich nun anschicke, diese Begriffe zu entwickeln, setze ich als Motto gleichsam den schon ausgesprochenen Grundsatz an die Spitze: Die Momente der Form sind nichts andres als die Bedingungen organischen Daseins und haben als solche keine Bedeutung für den Ausdruck. Sie geben nur das Schema des Lebendigen.

Regelmässigkeit wird definirt als: "Gleichmässige Wiederkehr unterschiedener, doch gleicher Teile." *Vischer* nennt als Beispiele: Säulen-ordnung, Folge eines dekorativen Musters, die gerade Linie, der Kreis, das Quadrat, etc.

Hier glaube ich zuerst, eine Ungenauigkeit rügen zu müssen: *Die Regelmässigkeit* der Abfolge muss entschieden getrennt werden von der "*Gesetzmässigkeit*" einer Linie, wie sie die Gerade, einer Figur, wie sie Quadrat und Kreis, oder nach dem Sprachgebrauch auch ein Winkel von 90° im Gegensatz zu einem von 80° zeigen.

Es ist nicht einzusehen, wie diese Dinge unter der einen Definition Platz finden sollten.

Der Unterschied zwischen Regelmässigkeit und dem, was ich hier einstweilen als Gesetzmässigkeit bezeichne, gründet sich auf eine sehr tiefgehende Differenz: *Hier* haben wir ein rein *intellektuelles* Verhältniss vor uns, *dort* ein *physisches.* Die Gesetzmässigkeit, die sich in einem <90° oder in einem Quadrat ausspricht, hat keine Beziehung zu unserm Organismus, sie gefällt nicht als eine angenehme Daseinsform, sie ist keine allgemein organische Lebensbedingung, sondern nur ein von unserm Intellekt bevorzugter Fall. Die Regelmässigkeit der Folge dagegen ist uns etwas Wertvolles, weil unser Organismus seiner Anlage gemäss nach Regelmässigkeit in seinen Funktionen verlangt. Wir atmen regelmässig, wir gehen regelmässig, jede andauernde Thätigkeit vollzieht sich in periodischer Folge. - Ein anderer Fall: Das eine Pyramide genau in einem <45° aufsteigt, bietet uns ein bloss intellektuelles Vergnügen, unserm Organismus ist dies gleichgültig, er rechnet bloss mit den Verhältnissen von Kraft und Schwere und gibt danach sein Urteil ab.

Es ist geboten, den prinzipiellen Unterschied dieser zwei Faktoren sich hier möglichst klar zu machen.

Ganz isolirt können sie wohl kaum je beobachtet werden, da jedes intellektuelle Verhältniss auch irgend eine physische Bedeutung hat und umgekehrt. Jedoch ist in der Verbindung der Anteil eines jeden meist unschwer zu erkennen.

Für die Charakteristik d. h. für den Ausdruck eines Kunstwerks ist der intellektuelle Faktor beinahe ganz bedeutungslos. Immerhin wird eine leicht erkennbare Ordnung den Reiz des Heiteren erhöhen, eine sehr complizirte, dem Intellekt unentwirrbare dagegen, indem *wir* beim Misslingen des Versuchs unmutig werden, selbst den Charakter dumpfen Unmuts anzunehmen scheinen. Wo endlich die Absicht allzu leicht erkannt wird, resultirt gewöhnlich ein öder, langweiliger Eindruck.

Wichtig ist der intellektuelle Faktor nur formal, weil er die *Selbstbestimmung* eines Objekts garantirt. Wo wir strenge Regel, verständliche Zahlen finden, da wissen wir: hier hat nicht der Zufall gewaltet, diese Form ist gewollt, das Objekt hat sich selbst bestimmt. (Natürlich kann das nur innerhalb der Grenzen des Physisch-Möglichen geschehen.) Interessant ist die Beobachtung, dass die älteste Kunst, der es vor allem darauf ankam, dem Zufall der Naturformen beabsichtigte, gewollte Gestalten entgegenzustellen, durch grelle Gesetzmässigkeit allein dies Ziel erreichen zu können glaubte. Es war einer späteren Zeit vorbehalten, auch in freieren Formen den Eindruck des Notwendigen zu wahren.

Symmetrie. Vischer definirt sie als "Gegen-überstellung gleicher Teile um einen trennenden Mittelpunkt, der ihnen ungleich ist. Man kann damit wohl einverstanden sein, sobald man sich nur darüber klar ist, dass hier nichts weiter gesagt sein soll, als dass bei *gegebenem* Mittelpunkt die Teile rechts und links gleich sein müssen. Die aktive Fassung der Definition verleitet zum Glauben, es sei in dem Begriff auch die *Aufstellung* eines Mittelpunkts eingeschlossen, was durchaus unrichtig ist, denn wo er fehlt, z. B. bei blosser Regel-mässigkeit, spricht man nicht von Asymmetrie.

Die Forderung der Symmetrie ist abgeleitet von der Anlage unseres Körpers. Weil wir symmetrisch aufgebaut sind, glauben wir diese Form auch von jedem architektonischen Körper verlangen zu dürfen. Nicht desswegen, weil wir unsern Gattungstypus als den unsrigen für den schönsten halten, wie man schon gemeint hat, sondern weil es uns so allein wohl ist.

In der Wirkung der Asymmetrie, von der gelegentlich schon gesprochen worden ist, liegt das Verhältniss klar vor; wir empfinden ein körperliches

Missbehagen; indem wir uns in der symbolisirenden Anschauung mit dem Objekt identifizirt haben, ist uns, als sei die Symmetrie unseres Leibes gestört, als sei ein Glied verstümmelt.

Aus dem Ursprung der Forderung von Symmetrie, ergibt sich auch ihre unbedingte Geltung. Man ist zwar oft der Meinung, der Zweckmässigkeit müsse sie sofort weichen, ohne dass das Gefallen eine Einbusse erlitte. *Fechner* (*Vorschule der Aesthetik*) bringt als Beispiel die Tasse, die ja nur *einen* Henkel habe. Allein gerade hier bewährt sich unser Prinzip auf's beste. Unwillkürlich wird uns die Henkelseite zum Rücken der Tasse, so dass die Sym-metrie gewahrt bleibt. Sobald dann 2 Henkel gegeben sind, dreht sich das Verhältnis wieder und wir fassen sie als ein Analogon unserer Arme.

Aus alldem geht aber auch zur Genüge hervor, dass ein Ausdruck in der Symmetrie als solcher nicht liegen kann, so wenig beim Menschen ein seelisches Moment in der Gleichheit der Arme zur Erscheinung kommt.

Mehr Schwierigkeiten macht die *Proportion*. Es ist das ein ganz unentwickelter Begriff. *Vischer's* Definition: Proportion setzt die Ungleichheit voraus und eine sie beherrschende Ordnung fest, sagt nicht viel, wie er selbst gesteht. Durch die Beifügung, sie gelte für die vertikale Richtung, ist nichts gewonnen, weil sie dann nicht mehr passt für Flächen (Verhältniss von h und b), wo man doch auch von Proportion spricht. Und wie von Höhe und Breite sagt man auch: die Träger müssen proportionirt sein zur Last.

Aus all diesen Fällen sieht man nur das eine: es handelt sich um das Verhältnis verschiedener Teile zu einander. Heissen diese *Kraft und Last*, so kann allein die Zweckmässigkeit entscheiden: der Träger muss seiner Aufgabe angemessen sein - das ist verständlich, ein physisches Prinzip.

Weiter müssen *Höhe* und *Breite* in einem "Verhältniss" zu einander stehen, 1:1 , 1:2, der goldne Schnitt sind solche Verhältnisse. Ich werde aber erst in dem Abschnitt vom Ausdruckswert der Proportion über diese Dinge handeln. Die Frage gehört nicht hieher, weil sie keine durchgehende notwendige und somit ausdruckslose Form betrifft.

Für den vertikalen Aufbau endlich eine zahlenmässige Ordnung als Hauptprinzip in Anspruch zu nehmen, ist ganz unpassend, denn hier tritt ein *qualitatives* Moment ein: die Durchformung des widerstrebenden Stoffes von unten nach oben. Bei der Symmetrie waren die Glieder qualitativ gleich. Hier sind die unteren Teile die schweren, gedrückten, die oberen die leichten, feiner Durchbildung zugänglichen. Zahlenverhältnisse, wie der (von Zeising überschätzte) goldne Schnitt, können darum hier als etwas sekundäres hinzutreten, vor allem aber verlangen wir jenen qualitativen Fortschritt von unten nach oben ausgedrückt zu sehen. Die Gesetze dieses Fortgangs entziehen sich aller mathematischen Bestimmbarkeit. - Ein Rustica-Geschoss von gleicher Höhe wie ein darüber liegendes zweites mit *glatter* Mauer, wirkt nicht als 1:1, die optische Fläche ist bei ungleichem Stoff nicht mehr entscheidend.

Das Prinzip ist auch hier dem organischen Aufbau entlehnt. In vollendetster Weise finden wir diese Entwicklung vom Rohen zum Feinem beim

Menschen. *Wundt* (*phys. Psych. II. 186*) macht darauf aufmerksam, dass eine Wiederholung homologer Teile stattfindet: "in den Armen und Händen wiederholen sich in feinerer und vollkommnerer Form die Beine und Füsse. Die Brust wieder-holt in gleichen Art die Form des Bauches. Während aber alle anderen Teile nur zweimal in der vertikalen Gliederung der Gestalt wiederholt sind, ist auf den Rumpf noch das Haupt gefügt, welches als der entwickeltste und allein in keinem andern homologen Organ vorgebildete Teil das Ganze abschliesst." - In diesem Prinzip der vertikalen Entwicklung ist der Architektur eine reiche Gelegenheit zur Charakteristik gegeben, aber das ist nicht mehr Proportion, keine formale, sondern eine inhaltliche Bestimmung. Darum hievon erst später.

Das letzte und geheimnissvollste Moment der Form ist die *Harmonie* als die "lebendig bewegte Einheit einer klar unterschiedenen Vielheit." - "Sie geht hervor aus der Einheit der inneren Lebenskraft. Sie bringt die Einheit in die Teile, weil sie die Teile ist" (Vischer).

Harmonie ist ein Begriff, den wir in voller Reinheit in der Morphologie als Definition von Organismus ausgebildet finden.

Das Individuum ist eine einheitliche Gemeinschaft, in welcher alle Teile zu einem gleichartigen Zwecke zusammenwirken (Einheit). Dieser Zweck ist ein innerer (Selbstbestimmung). Und der innere Zweck ist auch zugleich ein äusseres Mass, über welches die Entwicklung des Lebendigen nicht hinausreicht. (Form = innerer Zweck.)

Diese Sätze stammen von *Virchow*. Man kann sie unmittelbar in die Aesthetik herübernehmen.

Uebrigens hat schon *Kant* in anderem Zusammenhang dasselbe gesagt. Unter dem Titel "Architektonik der reinen Vernunft" gibt er eine vorzügliche Entwicklung dessen, was wir hier als Organismus und Harmonie bezeichnen. Er nennt es System.

Die Bestimmungen hierüber sind so treffend, dass ich sie in der Hauptsache hersetzen will.

Unter System ist zu verstehen die Einheit der mannigfaltigen Teile unter einer Idee. Diese Idee enthält den Zweck und die Form des Ganzen, das mit demselben kongruirt (d. h. Form = innerer Zweck). Die Einheit des Zwecks macht, dass kein Teil vermisst werden und keine zufällige Hinzusetzung stattfinden kann. Das Ganze ist also gegliedert und nicht gehäuft; es kann zwar innerlich, aber nicht äusserlich wachsen, wie *ein tierischer Körper,* dessen Wachstum kein Glied hinzusetzt, sondern ohne Veränderung der Proportion ein jedes zu seinen Zwecken stärker und tüchtiger macht. -

Damit ist alles gesagt, was vernünftiger Weise gewagt werden kann, und es ist, sehr bezeichnend, dass die Architektur den Namen für diesen Begriff gegeben hat.

Ein Ausdruck liegt in der Harmonie nicht. Sie bezeichnet nur das, was man mit einem andren Wort auch wohl die *Reinheit* der Formen genannt hat. Die Reinheit besteht eben darin, dass nicht Zufall sie geschaffen hat, die eine so, die andre so, sondern dass sie alle als Ausfluss einer zu Grunde liegenden Einheit erscheinen können und sich so als durchaus notwendig dokumentieren.

Der Eindruck des Organischen beruht, wie August *Thiersch* in der höchst lehrreichen Abhandlung über "Proportion" (*Handbuch der Architectur,* herausgegeben von *Durm* etc., Darmstadt IV. 1) nachgewiesen hat, hauptsächlich darauf, dass die gleiche Proportion im Ganzen und in den Teilen sich wiederholt. Es ist dasselbe Gesetz, das auch die Natur in ihren Bildungen befolgt.[7])

Damit haben wir die hauptsächlichen Formgesetze durchgegangen.

Wir treten den eigentlich ausdrucksvollen Elementen näher und behandeln also nacheinander.

1. die Verhältnisse der Höhe und Breite,
2. die horizontale Entwicklung,
3. die vertikale Entwicklung,
4. das Ornament.

4. Charakteristik der Proportionen

"Das Entscheidende in der Architektur sind die Maasse, die Verhältnisse von Höhe und Breite" (Hermann Grimm).

Sie bestimmen wesentlich den Charakter eines Bauwerks.

Es kommt mir darum sehr viel darauf an, den Ausdruckswert der Proportionen zu bestimmen.

Scheiden wir zuerst aus, was dem intellektuellen Faktor angehört: Proportionen wie 1:1, 1:2, 1:3 sind befried-igend, weil sie die Selbstbestimmung garantiren. Die Regel, die uns hier sofort entgegenleuchtet, überhebt uns der Frage: warum so? warum nicht anders? Die Form erscheint als eine notwendige. Darin kann aber ein

---

[7] Näher auf diese Dinge einzugehen, ist hier unmöglich, da der Gegenstand unbedingt die verdeutlichende Zeichnung erfordert.

Ausdruck noch nicht liegen.

Man erinnere sich an das, was wir früher über die mechanische Bedeutung aller Formverhältnisse sagten und man wird nicht widersprechen, wenn ich das Verhältnis von h und b, von Vertikale und Horizontale, dem Verhältniss von Ruhe und Streben gleichsetze, und darin den Ausdruckswert der Proportionen erkenne. Der physische Faktor ist also auch hier wieder das Charakteristische.

Wie aber stellt sich hiezu das vielberühmte Verhältnis des goldnen Schnittes? Ist das unbestreitbare Wohlgefallen, das dieser für sich hat, nach dem intellektuellen oder nach dem physischen Prinzip zu beurteilen? Was man von den Proportionen 1:1, 1:2, 1:3 gesagt hat, ihre ästhetische Bedeutung liege in der Leichtigkeit, womit wir diese einfachen Zahlen erkennen, findet hier offenbar keine Anwendung. Die grössere Seite ist nicht ein Vielfaches der kleinern, sondern h und b sind (arithmetisch ausgedrückt) irrational. Nun aber könnte man sich ja doch denken, das geometrische Verhältnis, dass die kleinere Seite zur grösseren sich verhalte, wie diese zum Ganzen, werde wahrgenommen. Jedoch, wo ist das Ganze? Ist es glaublich, dass wir in der Anschauung eines gold-geschnittenen Rechtecks b zu h hinzusetzen, um die Gerade zu gewinnen, die das Ganze repräsentirte?

Der intellektuelle Faktor scheint hier nicht zu passen.

Ein andres Bedenken gegen diese Erklärung ist dies, dass auch ein geschultes Auge nicht leicht den goldnen Schnitt als solchen erkennt. Bei 1:1 oder 1:2 werden Unvollkommenheiten sofort bemerkt, hier dagegen bleibt das Urteil in einer gewissen Breite schwankend. Die Zweifel mehren sich noch bei längerm Nachdenken; genug, ich glaube das Wohlgefallen muss aus den physischen Bedingungen erklärt werden, aus dem Verhältnis von Kraft und Schwere.

Man beobachte doch die Charakteristik der Scala der Proportionen.

Das ☐ heisst plump, schwerfällig, zufrieden, hausbacken, gutmütig, dumm u. s. f. Sein Eigentümliches liegt in der Gleichheit von h und b, Streben und Ruhe halten sich vollkommen das Gleichgewicht. Wir können nicht sagen, liegt der Körper oder steht er. Ein Ueberschuss von b würde ihn als ruhend, ein Ueberschuss von h als stehend erscheinen lassen. Dies ist nach dem allgemeinen Sprachgebrauch anerkannt. Mit grosser Consequenz sagen wir: dort *liegt* die Gemäldegalerie und hier *steht* der Turm.

Der Würfel gewinnt durch seine Indifferenz den Charakter absoluter Unbeweglichkeit. Er will nichts. Daher die Charakteristik: plump - gutmütig - dumm, ein Fortschreiten von körperlichen zu moralischen und schliesslich zu intellektuellen Eigenschaften.

Mit zunehmender Höhe verwandelt sich das Plumpe ins Fest-Gedrungene, geht über zum Elegant-Kräftigen, um schliesslich im Haltlos-Schlanken zu endigen, die Gestalt scheint dann der Unruhe ewigen Weiterwollens verfallen.

Umgekehrt, bei wachsendem b findet eine Entwicklung der Verhältnisse vom Klotzigen, Zusammengezogenen zu immer freierm Sich-Gehnlassen statt, das aber schliesslich in blosse zerfliessende Schwäche sich verliert; man bekommt den Eindruck, die Figur müsste ohne allen Halt immer mehr am platten

Boden sich ausbreiten.

(Diese Chakteristik ist, wie ich nebenbei bemerke, aus zahlreichen Experimenten mit Personen jeden Alters gewonnen worden.)

Aus alledem geht zur Genüge hervor, dass die Verhältnisse von h und b gedeutet werden auf Kraft und Schwere, Streben und Ruhe. Für den Ausdruck liegt in diesen Beziehungen ausserordentlich viel.

Was wir an uns selbst kennen, als behagliches Sich-Ausdehnen, ruhiges Gehn-Lassen, übertragen wir auf diese Art von Massenverteilung und geniessen die heitere Ruhe mit, die Gebärde solcher Art uns entgegenbringen. Umgekehrt kennen wir auch den Zustand des Gemütes, wenn man "sich usammennimmt", in kräftigernster Haltung sich aufrichtet u. s. w.

In der Skala der möglichen Combinationen scheint mir nun der goldene Schnitt desswegen eine bevorzugte Stellung einzunehmen, weil er ein Streben gibt, das sich nicht selbst verzehrt und in atemloser Hast nach oben drängt, sondern kräftiges Wollen mit ruhig festem Stand zu verbinden weiss. Das liegende goldgeschnittene Rechteck dagegen ist gleich weit entfernt von haltloser Schwäche und jenen klotzigen, dem □ sich nähernden Gestalten.

Der goldene Schnitt gäbe also in seinem Verhältnis von ruhigem Stoff und aufdrängender Kraft etwa *das demMenschen conforme Durchschnittsmass.* Ja, ich glaube beobachtet zu haben, dass schlanke Personen von unruhiger Beweglichkeit im Ganzen die schlankern Verhältnisse vorziehn, während kräftig untersetzte Leute umgekehrt wählen. Es wäre wünschenswert gewesen, dass *Fechner* bei seinen berühmten Experimenten hierauf Rücksicht genommen hätte.

Von den Dreiecksproportionen gilt das gleiche.

Von grossem lnteresse ist der Zusammenhang zwischen den Proportionen und dem *Tempo des Atmens*. Es ist kein Zweifel, sehr schmale Proportionen machen den Eindruck eines fast atemlos hastigen Aufwärtsstrebens. Und natürlich: es stellt sich sofort der Begriff des Engen ein, das uns keine Möglichkeit zu tiefem, seitliche Ausdehnung verlangendem Atemholen gewährt. So wirken die gothischen Proportionen beklemmend: für uns ist Raum genug zum Atmen da, aber in und mit diesen Formen lebend, glauben wir zu empfinden, wie sie sich zusammendrücken, aufwärtsdrängend, in sich selbst verzehrender Spannung. Die *Linien* scheinen mit gesteigerter *Schnelligkeit* zu laufen. Es mag hier als Beispiel, wie wenig die Bewegung der Augen für die Schnelligkeit des Linienflusses entscheidend ist, auf den Eindruck zweier Wellenlinien von ungleicher Schwingungsweite hingewiesen sein: kurze Schwing-ungen erscheinen uns rasch und flink, lange dagegen ruhig, oft müde: dort lebhaftes rasches Atmen- hier matte langsame Züge. Die Schwingungs- weite giebt die Dauer, die Schwingungs-höhe die Tiefe des Atemzuges an. Bei der Bedeutung des Tempos der Respiration für den Ausdruck von Stimmungen ist dieser Punkt für die historische Charakteristik sehr wichtig. Man kann die Beobachtung machen, dass Völker, ,je älter sie werden, desto rascher in ihrer Architektur anfangen zu atmen, sie werden aufgeregt. Wie still und ruhig laufen die Linien des alten dorischen Tempels: alles noch breit und langsamgemessen. Dann im Jonischen schon eine raschere Beweglichkeit, man sucht das Schlanke und Leichte, und je mehr die antike Kultur ihrem Ende nahe kam, desto mehr verlangte sie eine fieberhafte beschleunigte Bewegung. Völker, die von Hause aus ein rasches Blut haben, leisten dann das Höchste. Man denke an die erstickende Hast arabischer Dekorations linien. - Leider muss ich mich hier mit Andeutungen begnügen, eine historische Psychologie oder vielmehr eine psychologische Kunstgeschichte müsste die wachsende Schnelligkeit der Linienbewegung mit aller Exaktität verfolgen können und zwar wird sie finden, dass in der Dekoration der Fortschritt immer zuerst vor sich geht.

Uebrigens gibt es ausser der Flächenproportion noch andere Mittel, den Eindruck raschen Laufes hervor-zurufen. Ich muss aber hier beim Thema bleiben.

Die Proportionen sind das, was ein Volk als sein eigenstes gibt. Mag auch das System der Dekoration von aussen hineingetragen sein, in den Maassen von Höhe und Breite kommt der Volkscharakter immer wieder zum Durchbruch. Wer verkennt in der italienischen Gothik die nationale Vorliebe für weite, ruhige Verhältnisse und umgekehrt - bricht nicht im Norden immer wieder die Lust hervor am Hohen und Getürmten? Man könnte fast sagen, der Gegensatz von südlichem und nördlichem Lebensgefühl sei ausgedrückt in dem Gegensatz der liegenden und stehenden Proportionen. Dort Behagen am ruhigen Dasein, hier rastloses Fortdrängen. In der Geschichte der Giebelverhältnisse z. B. möchte man die ganze Entwicklung der Weltanschauungen wiederfinden. Ich fürchte nicht den Vorwurf, das seien Spielereien. Man ist zwar auch schon dahin gekommen, die engen gothischen Spitzbogen als ein blosses Resultat technischer Entwicklung anzusehen, und Leute, die mehr darin sehen wollten, als lächerliche Dilettanten zu behandeln. Aber man blicke doch auf den allgemeinen Zusammenhang, man sehe sich jene schlanken Menschen an, wie sie uns auf Gemälden der Zeit entgegentreten; wie ist da alles gestreckt, wie ist die Bewegung so zierlich steif, jeder einzelne Finger wie gespreizt! Was Wunder, wenn die Architektur auch scharf und spitz in die Höhe geht und die würdige Ruhe vergisst, die den romanischen Bauten eigen ist. Der Zusammenhang zwischen der Körperkonstitution und den bevorzugten Verhältnissen tritt hier deutlich hervor. Ob aber nun die physische Geschichte des menschlichen Körpers die Formen der Architektur bedingt oder von ihr bedingt ist, das ist eine Frage, die weiter führt, als wir hier zu gehn beabsichtigen.

Vielleicht ist schon im Verlauf der bisherigen Ausführungen das Bedenken wach geworden, ob man den überhaupt von *einem* Hauptverhältnis reden könne, es zeige ja doch jedes Gebäude eine Fülle mannigfacher Proportionen. Um solche Zweifel zu beschwichtigen, möchte ich versuchsweise den Begriff eines "*mittleren Verhältnisses*" einführen. Dass in der gothischen Architektur von solch einer durchgehenden Proportion gesprochen werden kann, muss jedermann zugeben, der Begriff hat aber auch für jeden anderen Stil seine Berechtigung. Er bezeichnet ganz analog dem "Mittelton" in der Musik, das Normale, die natürliche Ausdehnung, nach der dann die andren Proportionen moduliert werden und, unter steter Beziehung auf diese Norm, eben als Verengung oder Erweiterung wirken. Es findet also ein kombinatorischer Einfluss statt: die abweichenden Verhältnisse werden nicht für sich, sondern in einem ergänzenden Zusammen aufgefasst. Historisch lässt sich zeigen, dass die Combinationen zunehmen mit der reifenden Kunst. Die alte gibt lauter einfache, selbständige Verhältnisse.[8])

5. Charakteristik der horizontalen Gliederung

Das Prinzip der horizontalen Gliederung wird als *Symmetrie* bezeichnet. Symmetrie ist aber nur die Forderung, dass die Teile, die sich um einen ihnen ungleichen Mittelpunkt herumlegen, unter sich gleich sein müssen. Darin liegt, gar kein Ausdruck, wie ich schon oben gesagt habe, das Wichtige ist, *dass* sein Mittelpunkt dominierend sich heraushebt und dadurch abhängige Glieder um sich schafft. Wie die Geschichte der architektonischen Bildungen prinzipiell verwandt ist mit der Entwicklung der organischen Geschöpfe, so darf auch hier auf einen Satz der Morphologie hingewiesen werden: "Subordination der Teile deutet auf ein vollkommeneres Geschöpf. Je ähnlicher die Teile einander sind, desto weniger sind sie einander subordiniert." Der Fortschritt in der Entwicklung ist also eine Gliederung der Masse, die an sich stets in ihrer Ganzheit, zusammengeschlossen, verharren will.

---

[8] Die Gesetze dieser Modulationen aufzuweisen, gehört nicht hierher. Im übrigen verweise ich auf das zurück, was bei der Harmonie von durchgehenden Verhältnissen gesagt worden ist.

Die architektonische Bildung nähert sich damit der menschlichen Organisation und gewinnt die Fähigkeit, all das auszudrücken, was in dem Verhältnis der Glieder zum Körper vom Menschen gesagt werden kann. Das Charakteristische hiebei liegt in der grössern oder geringern Selbständigkeit dieser Teile. Resultiert das Gefühl der Freiheit überhaupt erst aus einer Entwicklung von Gliedern, die aus dem massigen Körper zu eignem Leben heraustreten, so wird die Wirkung um so fröhlicher, je freier die Verbindung mit dem Mittelbau. Wir finden hier jene Empfindung des Gelösten und Leichten wieder, die uns jede heitere Stimmung erregt. "So frei, so entlassen!" ruft *Vischer* einmal aus.

Eng angeschlossne Seitenteile dagegen, ohne selbständige Kraft, deuten auf unbedingte Abhängigkeit, auf vollständige Unterordnung unter den Willen der Mitte, gleich wie energisches Wollen beim Menschen in den eng am Körper anliegenden Gliedern sich ausspricht. Bei gegebenem Prinzip ist die Anwendung leicht zu machen und so brauche ich nicht die möglichen Fälle alle aufzuzählen. Das Prinzip ist uns durch unsere körperliche Organisation und unsere Ausdrucksbewegungen verständlich; in der Verwendung derselben ist die Architektur natürlich nicht mehr an die menschliche Analogie gebunden: sie kombiniert rein schematisch. -

Die symmetrische Gliederung oder die ungerade Teilung (3 =, 5 = Teilung) wenden wir an bei allem Selbständigen, da die hervorgehobene, den Teilen ungleiche Mitte eben den inneren Zusammenhalt repräsentiert, analog der Anlage unsres und jedes tierischen Organismus.

Gegen Zweiteilung haben wir eine entschiedene

Abneigung: es ist unorganisch, das Ding in der Mitte auseinanderfallen zu lassen.

Ein feines Gefühl aber hat die Zweiteilung für unselbständige Körper in Anwendung gebracht. Am griechischen Tempel z. B. ist die Vorderseite symmetrisch resp. ungerade geteilt, wir haben 5 oder 7 Interkolumnien (und auf diese, nicht auf die Säulen, kommt es an, da erst 2 Säulen zusammen etwas Selbständiges sind, gleich den 2 Beinen des menschlichen Körpers). Auf den Seiten dagegen finden wir eine gerade Zahl derselben, d. h. die Seite ist nichts selbständiges für sich: sie hat keine Mitte, die Mitte ist vielmehr durch ein tragendes Glied ausgefüllt.

Das Gleiche finden wir auch sonst in der Geschichte der Architektur. Der Erbauer der Villa Farnesina z. B. hat die Flügel der Fassade nur mit einer Zweiteilung bedacht und so fein ihre Unselbständigkeit gegenüber dem 5geteilten Mittelbau angedeutet.

Asymmetrie erscheint nur in leichten Fällen als Gleichgewichtsverschiebung, in schweren nötigt sie uns, jeden Teil als Individuum für sich aufzufassen und das Ganze mehr als eine zufällige Versammlung, denn als organische Verbindung zu nehmen.

Von monumentalen Gebäuden verlangen wir heutzutage unbedingte Symmetrie: würdige gemessene Haltung. Die Deutschen des Mittelalters und auch der Renaissance scheinen anders gedacht zu haben: sie rechneten darauf, dass jeder Teil an seinem Orte für sich wirken solle, auf das Ganze, das *uns* durch diese Ungebundenheit meist einen sehr muntern, durchaus nicht würdigernsten Eindruck macht, scheinen sie nicht

Rücksicht genommen zu haben. Wir dulden solche Freiheit nur noch an privaten oder ländlichen Gebäuden.

Ein eigentümliches Bedürfnis aber drängt unsre Zeit auch in ihrer häuslich-dekorativen Kunst zum Asymmet-rischen. Die Ruhe und Einfalt des stabilen Gleichgewichts ist langweilig geworden, man sucht mit Gewalt Bewegung, Aufregung, kurz die Zustände des Ungleichgewichts; man will nicht mehr den Genuss, wie Jacob *Burckhardt* einmal sagt, "sondern die Abspannung oder Zerstreuung und so ist entweder das Formloseste oder das Bunteste willkommen." - Wer will, mag sich in modernen Salons Beispiele zu diesem Satz suchen. Sie bieten sich reichlich.

Die moderne Vorliebe für das Hochgebirge, für mächtigste Massen ohne Regel und Gesetz, ist wohl zum Teil auf ein ähnliches Verlangen zurückzuführen.

Gleicherweise aber begreift es sich auch, dass eine gesteigerte Verletzung des Gleichgewichts schwermütig wirken kann. Wir selbst empfinden ja die Qual von Zuständen des Hangens und Bangens, wo die Ruhe des Gleichgewichts nicht gefunden werden kann. Ich möchte bei dieser Gelegenheit an einen Stich *Dürers* erinnern Melenconia I. Da sehn wir ein Weib in dumpfem Sinnen, hinstarrend auf einen Steinblock. Was soll das? Der Steinblock ist unregelmässig, irrational, er lässt sich nicht fassen mit Zirkel und Zahlen. Aber mehr. Man sehe diesen Stein an, scheint er nicht zu fallen? Gewiss. Und je länger man hinsieht, desto mehr wird man hineingezogen in diese Ruhelosigkeit; ein Würfel mit seinem absoluten Gleichgewicht mag langweilig sein, doch ist er befriedigt und befriedigend, hier aber tritt uns entgegen die qualvolle Unruhe dessen, was nicht die feste Form erreichen kann.

Die Körperhaltung bedingt Blut- zirkulation und Atem in ihrem Rhythmus. Und so führt uns die Betrachtung der Gleichgewichtszustände auf das, was man in der Architektur *Regelmässigkeit der Folge* oder Eurhythmie (Semper) genannt hat.

Ueber die Notwendigkeit des Regelmässigen für alles Lebendige haben wir schon gehandelt, ebenso über das Tempo, bei Gelegenheit der Proportionen.

Dass auch das *Unregelmässige* innerhalb der Schranken des schon Geformten bis zu gewissem Grad erlaubt ist, ergiebt die Analogie mit der Symmetrie und dem gemeinsamen Quell, der menschlichen atmenden Gestalt, die in ihrer Anlage symmetrisch, in ihren Funktionen regelmässig ist. Es gelten beiderseits die gleichen Bestimmungen: das Normale, Streng-Regelmässige kann durch eine Lockerung des Gesetzes den Charakter des Fröhlich-Freien, weiter aber auch des Unbefriedigten, Ruhelosen gewinnen. An monumentalen Gebäuden verlangen wir das Gleichmass der Regel unbedingt, dagegen wird eine leichte Unregelmässigkeit das Heitere ländlicher Anlagen noch erhöhn, sie muss aber sehr leicht sein, denn wir haben die Regelmässigkeit, gleich dem Takt in der Musik anzusehn, der zwar hie und da sich etwas dehnen lässt, im Ganzen aber doch als unverbrüderliches Grundgesetz gelten muss.

Von einem *Rhythmus* der Folge zu sprechen, scheint gewagt. Allein, weil wir nun doch einmal eine Folge unterschiedener Teile und damit, die Elemente des Taktes vor uns haben, warum sollte da nicht durch stärkere Betonung je des 2. oder 3. Teiles ein Rhythmus entstehn? Beispiel: Michaelskirche zu Hildesheim, wo auf zwei Säulen jedesmal ein Pfeiler folgt. Immerhin ist diese Art der Rhythmisirung eine ungewöhnliche; denn von einem stärkern Glied verlangen wir auch eine grössere Leistung, was hier nicht Fall der ist. Es bleibt aber noch eine andre Möglichkeit, da wir ja mehrere verschiedengliedrige Folgen n *übereinander* haben und die schwächern Glieder zwischen die stärkern sich einordnen müssen, wie leichte Begleitungsfiguren in der Musik dem langsamer fortschreitenden Hauptthema. In dem dadurch entstehenden Rhytmus ist in der That ein Moment von wesentlicher Bedeutung gegeben, das beim Eindruck des Ganzen eine nicht zu unterschätzende Rolle spielt.

Nehmen wir die griechische Tempelarchitektur:

Die Säulen sind unter sich alle gleich, die darüber-liegenden Triglyphen sind es ebenfalls; ob aber 2 oder 3 Triglyphen auf eine Säule kommen, mit anderen Worten, ob der Raum zwischen je zwei Säulen in $2/2$ oder $3/3$ geteilt wird, das macht den Rhythmus aus. Der der Säule entsprechende Triglyphenschlitz wird nämlich unmittelbar als der stärker betonte erscheinen.

Die Wirkung in beiden Fällen ist eine durchaus verschiedene. Wo eine Triglyphe in den Schwerpunkt des Gebälkstücks fällt, also genau in die Mitte des Inter-kolumniums, da resultiert für uns der Eindruck strenger Gebundenheit, anderenfalls, wo dieser Punkt unbezeichnet bleibt, wirkt die freiere Ordnung leicht und fröhlich. Das ist nun allerdings noch keine genügende Erklärung. Man thut vielleicht gut, an die Bedeutung des $4/4$ und ¾ Takt, für unsre Bewegung zu erinnern: Wir marschieren leichter im ¾ Takt. Der betonte Tritt fällt dann nicht immer demselben Fusse zu, sondern wechselt ab, der Gang wird leicht und schwebend.[9])

Ich verzichte darauf, weitere Fälle anzuführen: allgemein lässt sich sagen, dass der alten, strengen Kunst nur die Zweiteilung entspricht. Die griechischrömische Architektur hat erst spät das Reizmittel - wenn ich so sagen darf - des ¾ Taktes angewendet. Ich finde es zuerst am Rundtempel zu Tivoli.

Die grösste Ungebundenheit zeigt sich dann darin, dass die Rhythmen verschiedener Reihen nicht mehr zusammenklingen. So bei vielen Gebäuden der Renaissance z. B. Tempietto bei San Pietro in Montorio (Rom) oder Vorhalle von S. Maria (Arezzo) u. s. w.

6. Charakteristik der vertikalen Gliederung

Wir haben die zunehmende Durchformung des Stoffes als das Prinzip des vertikalen Aufbaus erkannt.

Beim Menschen besteht diese Durchformung in der Bildung feinerer Organe, die sowohl am Körper sich freier bewegen können als auch selbst, in sich, mannigfaltiger gegliedert sind. Man vergleiche in dieser Hinsicht Beine und Arme.

Weiter ist es gleichsam eine Durchbrechung der geschlossenen Masse, die uns in den Augen z. B. entgegentritt.

---

[9] Denkbar wäre aber auch, dass wir, das Moment der Folge aufgebend, zur Erklärung das beiziehen müssten, was wir oben über Zwei und Dreiteilung gesagt haben. Es ist mir unmöglich, mich zu entscheiden, da mannigfache Beobachtungen und Versuche kein bestimmtes Resultat ergaben.

Was entspricht dem in der Architektur? Sie gliedert ihren Stoff in gleicher Weise und durchbricht die Mauer mit Oeffnungen. Die Oeffnungen nehmen zu an Grösse, die Gliederungen werden feiner, die Organe selbständiger. Der Träger, der zuerst als Mauerpfeiler erschien, kann zur freien Säule werden mit eigenem Sockel. Doch will ich nicht auf einzelnes eingehn, es kommt mir nur auf das Prinzip an: auf die Entfaltung der vertikal wirkenden Formkraft.

Diese Kraft stellt sich uns dar als die gleiche in Säulen und Fenstern und Gesimsen. Ueberall der Zug nach oben, der der Schwere sich entgegenstemmt und in einer konoiden Form gewöhnlich seinen Abschluss sucht. Unten also haben wir alles massiv, ungegliedert, ungebrochen: es ist die Basis, der Sockel; die ganze Wucht des Schweren kommt hier zur Geltung. Ein Rustika-Erdgeschoss gestattet nur ganz kleine Fensteröffnungen und auch hier scheint die Gefahr nicht ausgeschlossen zu sein, dass die Masse sie verschlingt, indem sie sich wieder zusammenzieht. Das ist uns wohl verständlich, beleidigt unser Gefühl nicht. Fehlen dagegen die Oeffnungen oben, verharrt der Stoff in seiner ungegliederten Ganzheit, so erscheint uns das Wesen als blind, als befangen in dumpfem Dasein.[10])

---

[10] Hr. Prof. v. *Brunn* macht mich auf ein scheinbar widersprechendes Beispiel aufmerksam: auf den Dogenpalast in Venedig, zugleich mit dem Bemerken, dass diese Ausnahme die Regel bestätige. Hier haben wir nämlich allerdings über den Hallen der untern Geschosse eine mächtige Obermauer mit nur wenig Fenstern, jedoch diese Obermauer ist schon gemustert d. h. mit Formelementen durchzogen und wirkt darum nicht schwer; weiterhin aber - und dies ist wohl noch bedeutsamer - wird sie nicht durch ein Kranzgesims abgeschlossen, sondern löst sich in ein spitzenartiges Ornament auf.

Die Architektur nähert sich hier der menschlichen Organisation in sehr bedeutender Weise, so dass sich physiognomische Analogien mit grosser Entschiedenheit einstellen. Wir sind gewohnt den freisten Ausdruck da zu finden, wo ein Teil dem mechanischen Druck enthoben ist: so spricht beim Tier der Schwanz am deutlichsten, beim Menschen der Kopf und in der Architektur, die ebenfalls eine Richtung nach oben hat und gerade aussieht (nicht zu Boden wie das Tier oder aufwärts wie die Pflanze), sind die ausdrucksvollsten Teile entsprechend auch die obern. Hieher wendet sich unwillkürlich unser Blick. Hier liegt für uns die Charakteristik, die für das ganze übrige Gebäude bestimmend wird.

Unserer Phantasie genügt dabei der leiseste Anstoss, sie hält sich an ein einzelnes und verlangt durchaus keine Entsprechung im weitern. So wenig Aehnlichkeit daher auch ein Haus mit einer menschlichen Gestalt hat, wir finden doch in den Fenstern Organe, die unsern Augen ähnlich sind. Man sagt, sie "vergeistigen" den Bau. Und ihnen kommt daher der ganze Ausdruckswert zu, der in der Stellung des Auges zu seiner Umgebung liegt. Der Teil über den Fenstern wird uns zur Stirn. Heiterkeit verlangt eine glatte Stirn. Rustika-Behandlung wirkt, sehr düster an dieser Stelle, namentlich wenn der Raum nicht hoch ist. So können wir uns beim Finanzministerium in München des Eindrucks nicht erwehren, dass es die Stirne runzle, ein Palazzo Strozzi dagegen wirkt durch seine höhere Obermauer trotz Rustika nicht unmutig, sondern nur ernst bedeutsam. Scheinen die Fenster unmittelbar beschattet von einem vorstehenden Kranzgesims, so gewinnen wir den Eindruck, als wären die Brauen zusammengezogen und den Augen als schützendes Ueberdach gleichsam vor- geschoben.

Es wäre eine nicht undankbare Aufgabe die physio-gnomischen Möglichkeiten, die die Architektur verkörpern kann, zusammenzustellen. Bei all dem kommt es natürlich nur auf das P r i n z i p an, es liegt durchaus nicht die Absicht *menschliche* Gesichtszüge nachzuahmen. Vielleicht verliert auch die Idee einer architektonischen Physiognomik einigermassen ihr befremdendes, wenn man bedenkt, dass die menschlichen Ausdrucksbewegungen in den Gesichtsmuskeln denen des ganzen Körpers immer ähnlich sind; so ziehen wir mit den Augenbrauen gleichzeitig die Schultern in die Höhe, mit vertikaler Stirnfaltung verbindet sich Steifung des ganzen Körpers, wer die Brauen über die Augen verschiebt, senkt auch den Kopf gegen die Brust vor. Daraus erklärt sich die Bedeutung des Prinzips auch in aussermenschlicher Verwendung wohl hinlänglich.

So viel in Kürze über den Gegenstand, der im folgenden Abschnitt noch deutlicher werden wird.

Bevor wir aber übergehn zum Ornament, muss noch auf ein Moment in der Charakteristik der Vertikalkraft hingewiesen werden.

Form ist That. Jedes Fenster muss in jedem Augenblick gegen den Druck der Materie sich behaupten.

Verschiedene Zeiten haben dies Verhältnis verschieden aufgefasst.

Der Rundbogen ist anerkanntermassen fröhlicher als der Spitzbogen: jener lebt sich ruhig aus - gesättigte

Rundung; dieser ist in jeder Linie Wille, Anstrengung, nie ruhend scheint er die Mauer immer noch höher hinauf spalten zu wollen.

Mit dem Bestreben, in jeder Form den Ausdruck konzentrierten Wollens zu geben, verbindet sich bei der *Gothik* eine Abneigung gegen allen Stoff, der stumpf und breit da liegt. Alles Träge, Haltlose ist ihr unleidlich; was sie mit ihrem Willen nicht durch und durchdringen kann, muss verschwinden. So kommt es zu einer gänzlichen Auflösung aller Masse, die Horizontale weicht und im unaufhaltsamen Emporfahren befriedigt sich der Drang, befreit von aller Schwere, hochhinauf die Luft zu durchschneiden.

Den ganzen Bau in funktionierende Glieder auflösen, heisst: jeden Muskel seines Körpers fühlen wollen. Das ist der eigentliche Sinn der Gotik. Ich komme später nochmals darauf zurück. Wo immer dieser Drang in der Geschichte sich findet, ist er ein Symptom hoher Aufregung.

Die heitere Ruhe des klassischen Zeitalters kennt nichts dergleichen. In der griechischen Architektur ist dem Stoff ein weiter Spielraum gelassen, das Gebälk lastet mit bedeutender Schwere und in der geringen Höhe des Giebels zeigt sich der nur mässige Ueberschuss der Vertikalkraft. Der Grieche suchte nicht das Stoffliche abzustreifen, er freut sich der Kraft, die ihren Widerstand findet, ohne darin eine Beeinträchtigung zu sehen und ein unbehindertes zweckloses Aufstreben zu verlangen.

Für den modernen Geist ist es bezeichnend, dass er gerne in der Architektur die Form sich mühsam aus dem Stoff herausarbeiten lässt, er will nicht das Fertige, sondern das Werdende sehen, den allmäligen Sieg der Form.

Die Rustika der Renaissance hat diesen Gedanken deutlich zum Ausdruck gebracht. Weiterhin wurde vom Barockstil das Motiv bis zu dem Extrem verfolgt, dass die Form aus dem rohen Felsgestein sich herauswinden muss.

Die Antike stellte das Vollkommene gleich rein und ganz hin, als könnte es nicht anders sein.

Auf theoretischem Gebiet könnte man als Beispiel zu diesem tiefgehenden Unterschied zwischen antiker und moderner Anschauung gegenüberstellen: *Lessing* mit seinem bekannten Wort: "Lass mich irren, nur lass mich forschen" und *Aristoteles* (*Nic. Eth.* 1177 a 26): εὔλογον δέ τοῖς εἰδόσι των ζητούντων ἡδίω τήν διαγωγήν εἶναι.

7. Das Ornament

Nur mit Mühe hat bisher die Erörterung des Ornaments zurückgeschoben werden können. Es trägt zur Charakteristik der horizontalen, noch mehr aber der vertikalen Entwickelung ausserordentlich viel bei. Doch schien mir eine zusammenhängende Behandlung des Themas vorzuziehen.

Was ist das Ornament? Die Lösung der Frage ist dadurch vielfach getrübt worden, dass man, wie Bötticher in seiner Tektonik der Hellenen, nach der kanonischen Bedeutung jedes Teiles fragte, ein geschlossenes System aufsuchen zu müssen glaubte oder aber mit der Frage nach der historischen Entstehung einer Form sich abquälte.

Ich bin in einer glücklicheren Lage, indem ich nur das eine wissen will: *Wie wirkt* das Ornament? Wagner (*Handbuch der Arch.* IV. 1, 31 ff.) unterscheidet in üblicher Weise dekoratives und konstruktives Ornament, weiss aber von dem dekorativen nichts mehr zu sagen, als dass es "in sinniger Weise tote Flächen und starre Gliederungen beleben solle," während er dem konstruktiven die Aufgabe gibt, "die durch den Stil bedingte Kunstform des Strukturteils zu heben und zu schmücken."

Mit dieser Erklärung ist nicht viel zu machen. Schon die Unterscheidung von dekorativ und konstruktiv ist von zweifelhaftem Wert. Man stösst bei der Anwendung sofort auf Bedenken und findet, dass die Grenze eine fliessende sei. Jedenfalls empfiehlt es sich nicht davon auszugehen und so nehme ich das Ornament als ganzes und stelle den Satz auf, den ich nachher erproben will: *Das Ornament ist Ausdruck über schüssiger Formkraft.* Die schwere Masse treibt keine Blüten.

Versuchen wir den Wert dieser Erklärung zuerst an einem dorischen Tempel.

Die ganze untere Hälfte, vom Kapitell abwärts zeigt keine dekorativen Formen: weder Tempelstufen noch Säulenstamm würden eine Verzierung ertragen: dort haben wir die rohe Masse, schwer daliegend, kaum der einfachsten Form gewonnen, hier im Säulenstamm erwarten wir Anstrengung, konzentrierte Kraft, was die Kanellüren deutlich zum Ausdruck bringen; eine skulpirte Säule hätte den Charakter des Sich-Zusammennehmens vollständig verloren. Vom Kapitell wollen wir nachher reden. Was kommt über den Säulen? Das Gebälk, die zu tragende Last, eine mächtige Horizontale. Wäre die Last grösser, so müssten die Säulen in der Mitte ausweichen, die Horizontale würde dominieren. Aber umgekehrt: die Vertikalkraft ist mächtiger, sie durchdringt die Schwere, erst nur leise, der Architrav verbleibt noch in ungebrochener Ganzheit und nur in den Schilden über den Säulen manifestirt sich die Wirkung des Stosses; dann nach Ueberwältigung dieses ersten Widerstandes wird die Last leichter, die Kraft bricht durch: es erscheinen in den Triglyphen vertikale Glieder, die das Kanellürenmotiv der Säulen wieder aufnehmen und in den zwischengestellten Metopen bekundet sich schon ein tektonisch-unabhängiges Leben: es ist Raum geschaffen zur Entfaltung feinster Gebilde und wenn endlich die Mutuli die ganze Breite des Gebälks ausfüllen, so macht dies den Eindruck, als klinge hier der Säulenstoss sanft aus, nachdem er sich über das ganze Gebälk ausgedehnt. Es folgt die höchste That: die Schwere ist überwunden, der Ueberschuss der strebenden Kraft erscheint in der *Hebung* [11]) des Giebels und feiert den höchsten Triumph in den plastischen Figuren, die, dem Druck enthoben, hier frei sich entfalten können. [12])

---

[11] Vischer fragt einmal, ob der Giebel steige oder sich niedersenke. Beides. Er wird in der Mitte gehoben; Ausdruck dessen: Der Firstziegel; und die Seitenlinien fliessen abwärts, denn in den (seitwärts blickenden) *Akroterien* beugt die hier sich entwickelnde Kraft sich zurück. (Je steiler der Giebel, desto bedeutender müssen diese Akroterien sein.) Die Gothik dagegen zeigt in den *Krabben* eine überschüssige Vertikalkraft.

[12] Es liesse sich vielleicht auch eine Correspondenz zwischen den Giebelfiguren und der Ordnung der Triglyphen konstatiren. Ich habe das nicht untersucht. Nur bemerke ich z. B. beim Tempel der Aegineten eine solche Entsprechung: 11 Triglyphen - 11

Nun aber, wenn man das auch zugibt, so wird man im Kapitell einen Widerspruch finden, indem man sagen kann, dort erscheine nicht ein Ueberschuss von Kraft, sondern im Gegenteil eine Pressung der Säule. Das ist aber unrichtig. Und wenn Bötticher in dem aufgemalten Blätterkranz, der von dem Druck niedergebeugt scheine, den Gedanken rein dargestellt; findet, so darf ich wohl demgegenüber das Recht des unmittelbaren Eindrucks geltend machen. Hier weisen die Blätter keineswegs auf Pressung, sie blühen ganz ruhig aus dem Echinus heraus. Was wäre das auch für eine Leistung, wenn das Gewicht des ganzen Gebälkes ein paar Blätter hätte umbeugen können. Das Motiv ist lächerlich klein. Kurz, mir scheint, die Blätter haben nichts zu thun bei dem Konflikt jener gewaltigen Massen, sondern sind möglich allein deswegen, weil eben die Belastung das freie Leben der Säule nicht tötet.

Es ist wichtig, sich klar zu machen, dass eine Pressung niemals ästhetisch wirksam sein kann. Selbstbestimmung ist das erste Gebot. Jede Form muss zureichender Grund von sich selbst sein. Und so ist es auch hier der Fall. Die Säule breitet sich oben aus, weil es zweckmässig ist, die Last breit zu fassen, nicht weil sie gequetscht wird;[13]) sie behält immer noch Kraft genug, sich unmittelbar unter dem Abacus) wieder zusammen zu ziehen. Und eben in dem Mass, wie weit sie in der Ausbreitung geht, liegt die Garantie ihrer Selbstbestimmung. Sie geht so weit als der Abacus reicht.

Figuren. - Ueber den frappanten Zusammenhang zwischen Architektur und Composition der "pergamenischen Gigantomachie" vgl. Brunn in seinem Aufsatz pag. 50. Berlin 1885.

[13] Ein elastisches Nachgeben ist damit natürlich nicht geläugnet.

Der Abacus aber ist - und nun staune man das architektonische Feingefühl der Griechen an - dieser Abacus ist das proportionale Abbild des ganzen Gebälks. D. h. die Säule weiss genau, was sie zu tragen hat und handelt demgemäs.

In der jonischen Architektur macht sich, wie wir schon bemerkten, ein Streben nach freierer Beweglichkeit geltend. Man will auch nicht mehr so schwer tragen. Die Säule wird entlastet und der leichtere Eindruck dadurch hauptsächlich erzielt, dass man sie sich in den Voluten einer überschüssigen Kraft entledigen liess (was bei der dorischen Säule ohne Bemalung nicht der Fall ist). Bei vergleichender Beurteilung von dorischen und jonischen Säulen hatte ich oft Gelegenheit zu hören: die jonische halte den Kopf frei aufrecht, die dorische habe ihn gesenkt. Die Alten scheinen selbst diesen Eindruck gehabt zu haben, wenn man wenigstens die Telamonen von Akragas und die Karyatiden des Erechtheion als dorisch und jonisch bezeichnen darf. Ich glaube man ist dazu berechtigt. Ja, es ist mir vorgekommen, dass von einer Person die weder Telamonen noch Karyatiden gesehen hatte, die dorische Säule mit ihrem Echinus durch ganz ähnliches Ausbreiten der Ellbogen und Senken opfes charakterisiert wurde und ebenso die Voluten der jonischen Säulen als herabfallende Haare einer voll aufgerichteten Gestalt bezeichnet wurden.

Man kann das Verhältnis der zwei Stile durch ein treffliches Wort Goethes illustrieren (aus dem Aufsatz über Baukunst von 1788): "Es ist in der menschlichen Natur, immer weiter, ja über ihr Ziel fortzuschreiten und so ist es auch natürlich, dass in dem Verhältnis der Säulendicke zur Höhe das Auge immer das Schlankere suchte und der Geist *mehr Hoheit und Freiheit* dadurch zu empfinden glaubte."

Mehr Hoheit und Freiheit! Das ist der Drang, der auch aus dem romanischen Stil zu den gothischen Formen überführte. Ich kann in diesen Prolegomenis, die ja immer nur andeutend sich verhalten sollen, nicht auf eine Analyse dieser Dekorationen eingehen. Bei gegebenem Prinzip macht das aber keine Schwierigkeiten. Man wird leicht erkennen, dass das ganze Feuerwerk gothischer Ornamentik nur möglich ist durch den enormen Ueberschuss der Formkraft über den Stoff. Ornament ist das Ausblühen einer Kraft, die nichts mehr zu leisten hat. Es ist ein sehr richtiges Gefühl gewesen, das Kapitell umzuwandeln in einen leicht umkränzenden Blätter-schmuck, denn der gotische Pfeiler saust nach oben ohne irgendwo seine Kraft zu zersplittern. Ebenso richtig empfunden war es später aber auch in der italienischen Renaissance, dass die Säule, die einen Bogen trägt, diesen nicht unmittelbar über ihrem Kapitell darf ansetzen lassen, sondern ein Gebälkstück zwischen hineintreten muss, an dem sich die Säule brechen kann, wie ein Wasserstrahl an einem Widerstand sich bricht. Es beweist die tiefe architektonische Einsicht Brunellescos, dass er diese Notwendigkeit erkannte, es beweist aber auch, dass unsere These nicht aus der Luft gegriffen ist, sondern an den entscheidenden Punkten sich bewährt.

Ich darf darum hoffen, man verlange hier keine weiteren Analysen und so beschliesse ich diesen Abschnitt[14]) mit einer historischen Betrachtung.

---

[14] Eine sekundäre Quelle der Ornamentik besitzt die Architektur in dem "angehängten" Schmuck d. h. in Ring und Behang, Land u. dgl. Dieser ist nicht eigentlich architektonisch zu nennen, denn er ist eine

Reife Kulturen verlangen stets einen grossen Ueberschuss der Formkraft über den Stoff. Die ruhige Wirkung geschlossener Mauermassen wird unerträglich. Man verlangt Bewegung, Aufregung, wie wir schon zu bemerken Gelegenheit hatten. In Bezug auf Dekoration resultiert eine Kunst, die dem nachfühlenden Sinne nirgends mehr stille Flächen gewährt, sondern von jedem Muskel ein zuckendes Leben verlangt. So in der Gothik, im Arabischen und - unter ganz anderen architectonischen Bedingungen - die gleichen Symptome auch im alternden Rom. Man "belebt" alle Flächen mit Nischen, Wandsäulen etc., nur um der Aufregung Ausdruck zu geben, die den eigenen Körper durchwühlt und an ruhigem Dasein kein Genüge mehr finden lässt.

8. Prinzipien der historischen Beurteilung

Wir haben bisher den Menschen nach seinen allgemeinen Verhältnissen als massgebend für die Architektur erkannt; es darf dies Prinzip noch weiter ausgedehnt werden: ein architektonischer Stil gibt die *Haltung* und *Bewegung der Menschen* seiner Zeit wieder. Im Kostüm kommt zuerst die Art zum Ausdruck, wie man sich halten und bewegen will und es ist nicht schwer zu zeigen, dass die Architektur mit dem

---

Uebertragung der Art, wie man die *fertige menschliche* Gestalt ziert. Er wirkt auch in ganz gleicher Weise wie hier, nämlich vermittelst Tastempfindungen. Ringumschlossne Säulen z. B. erregen dieselben Gefühle wie ein Arm, dessen fleischige Teile ein Band umfasst. Nach der meisterhaften Entwicklung der Prinzipien des Schmucks, die Lotze im *Microcosmos* gegeben hat (II[3] 203 ff), brauche ich hierüber nichts weiter zu sagen.

Zeitkostüm übereinstimmt. Ich möchte auf dieses Prinzip der historischen Charakteristik um so energischer hinweisen, je weniger ich hier im stande bin, den Gedanken eingehend zu verwerten.

Als Beispiel diene der gothische Stil.

Lübke erkennt in ihm den Ausdruck des Spiritualismus. *Semper* nennt ihn die lapidare Scholastik. Nach welchen Prinzipien hat man geurteilt? Das tertium comparationis ist nicht eben deutlich, wenn auch jede Bezeichnung etwas richtiges treffen mag. Einen festen unkt gewinnen wir erst durch Reduktion dieser psychischen Dinge auf die menschliche Gestalt.

Der Drang nach dem Präzisen, Scharfen, Willensbewussten ist die geistige Thatsache, die vorliegt. Die Scholastik zeigt sehr klar diese Abneigung gegen alles Unbestimmte, die Begriffe werden zu höchster Präzision ausgearbeitet.

Körperlich stellt sich dies Streben dar als exakteste Bewegung, Zuspitzung aller Formen, kein Gehenlassen, nichts Schwammiges, überall bestimmtester Ausdruck eines Willens.

Scholastik und Spiritualismus können der Gothik als Ausdruck nur zugeschrieben werden, wenn man dies Mittelglied im Auge behält, wo ein Psychisches sich unmittelbar in körperliche Form umsetzt. Der spitzfindige Feinsinn der scholastischen Jahrhunderte und der Spiritualismus, der keinen dem Willen entzogenen Stoff duldet, können allein durch ihren körperlichen Ausdruck für die architektonische Formgebung bedeutsam geworden sein.

Hier finden wir die gothischen Formen im Prinzip gegeben: Der Nasenrücken wird feiner, die Stirn legt sich in senkrechte, harte Falten, der ganze Körper steift sich, nimmt sich zusammen, alle ruhige Breite schwindet. Es ist bekannt, dass viele Leute (namentlich Dozenten) zum scharfen Denken eines scharfkantigen Bleistifts benötigen, den sie zwischen den Fingern hin und her drehen und an diesen Tastgefühlen ihr Denken stärken. Ein runder Bleistift würde diese Stelle nicht versehen können. Was will das Runde? Man weiss es nicht. Und so auch der romanische Rundbogen, er lässt keinen bestimmten Willen erkennen. Er steigt wohl empor, aber erst im Spitzbogen findet dies Streben einen deutlichen Ausdruck.

Der menschliche Fuss hat eine Richtung nach vorn, aber tritt das in der stumpfen Linie, in der er aufhört, hervor? Nein. Es war der Gothik unleidlich, hier nicht den exakten Ausdruck eines Willens zu finden und so liess sie den Schuh in spitzem Schnabel auslaufen. (Die Schnabelschuhe erscheinen im XII. Jahrh., vgl. Weiss, *Kostümkunde* IV. 8.)

Die Breite der Sohle ist eine Folge der Schwere des Körpers. Aber der Körper hat kein Recht, er ist Stoff und dem dummen Stoff darf nicht nachgegeben werden, der Wille muss jeden Teil durchdringen können.

Darum löst die Architektur die Mauer auf in vertikale Glieder und die menschliche Sohle bekommt einen Schuh mit drei hohen Absätzen, wodurch das Gefühl breiten Auftretens beseitigt ist.

Ich will nicht verfolgen, wie in den spitzen Hüten das Prinzip des Giebels sich zeigt, wie die Bewegungen alle so steif, zierlich oder auch so schneidig und präzis sind, wie schliesslich (woran ich schon erinnert habe) die Körper selbst gestreckt und überschlank erscheinen[15] - ich bin zufrieden, wenn verständlich geworden ist, was ich meine.

Man durchwandert mit Erstaunen die Geschichte und beobachtet, wie die Architektur überall das Ideal des Menschen in Körpergestalt und Körperbewegung nachgebildet, wie selbst grosse *Maler* für ihre Menschen eine entsprechende Architektur geschaffen haben. Oder pulst etwa in den Bauformen eines Rubens nicht das gleiche Leben, das seine Körper durchströmt!

Ich schliesse ab. Eine vollständige Psychologie der Architektur zu geben, war nicht meine Absicht, rein aber und ganz wünschte ich, dass der Gedanke zur Erscheinung käme: es werde ein organisches Verständnis der Formengeschichte erst dann ermöglicht sein, wenn man weiss, mit welchen Fasern der menschlichen Natur die Formphantasie zusammenhängt.

Der Historiker, der einen Stil zu beurteilen hat, besitzt kein Organon zur Charakteristik, sondern ist nur auf ein instinktives Ahnen angewiesen.

Das Ideal, "exakt zu arbeiten," schwebt auch den historischen Disziplinen vor. Die Kunstgeschichte sucht darum vor allem die verderbliche Berührung mit der Aesthetik zu vermeiden und mancherorts bestrebt man sich, nur noch zu sagen, was nacheinander gewesen sei und kein Wort mehr. So wenig ich geneigt bin, das Gute dieser Tendenz zu verkennen, so muss ich doch glauben, die höchste Stufe der Wissenschaft sei damit nicht erreicht. Eine Geschichte, die nur immer konstatieren will, was nacheinander gekommen ist, kann nicht bestehen; sie würde sich namentlich täuschen, wenn

---

[15] Man darf freilich nicht vergessen, dass Gemälde und noch mehr Skulpturen keine sichere historische Quelle hiefür sind.

sie glaubte, dadurch "exakt" geworden zu sein. Man kann erst da exakt arbeiten, wo es möglich ist, den Strom der Erscheinungen in festen Formen aufzufangen. Diese festen Formen liefert der Physik z. B. die Mechanik. Die Geisteswissenschaften entbehren noch dieser Grundlage; sie kann allein in der Psychologie gesucht werden. Diese würde auch der Kunstgeschichte erlauben, das einzelne, auf ein allgemeines, auf Gesetze zurückzuführen. Die Psychologie ist zwar weit entfernt von dem Zustand der Vollkommenheit, wo sie sich der geschichtlichen Charakteristik als ein Organon anbieten könnte, aber ich halte das Ziel nicht für unerreichbar.

Man könnte der Idee einer solchen Kunst-psychologie, die vom Eindruck, den wir empfangen, zurückschliesst auf das Volksgefühl, das diese Formen, diese Proportionen erzeugte, man könnte ihr den Einwurf machen: Schlüsse der Art seien unberechtigt, Verhältnisse und Linien bedeuteten nicht immer dasselbe, das menschliche Formgefühl verändere sich.

Der Einwurf ist nicht zu widerlegen, solange man keine psychologische Basis hat; sobald aber die Organisation des menschlichen Körpers als der bleibende Nenner bei allem Wechsel erwiesen ist, ist man gegen diesen Schlag gesichert, indem die Gleichförmigkeit dieser Organ-isation auch die Gleichförmigkeit des Formgefühls verbürgt.

Dass weiterhin Stil-Formen nicht von Einzelnen nach Belieben gemacht werden, sondern aus dem Volksgefühl erwachsen, dass der Einzelne nur dann mit Erfolg schöpferisch thätig sein kann, wenn er untergegangen ist im Allgemeinen, wenn er den Volks- und Zeitcharakter vollkommen repräsentiert, ist zu allgemein bekannt, um noch weiterer Ausführungen zu bedürfen; bleibt aber auch das Formengefühl seiner Qualität nach unverändert, so darf man doch die Schwankungen seiner Intensität nicht verkennen. Es hat wenige Zeiten gegeben, die jede Form rein verstanden d. h. miterlebten. Es sind nur die Perioden, die sich ihren eigenen Stil geschaffen haben.

Da aber die grossen Formen der Baukunst nicht jedem leisen Wandel des Volksgemüts nachgeben können, so tritt eine allmählige Entfremdung ein, der Stil wird zum leblosen Schema, behauptet sich nur noch durch Tradition. Die einzelnen Formen werden unverstanden fortgebraucht, falsch verwendet und so gänzlich abgetötet.

Den Pulsschlag der Zeit muss man anderswo belauschen: in den kleinen dekorativen Künsten, in den Linien der Dekoration, den Schriftzeichen[16]) u. s. f. *Hier befriedigt sich das Formengef*ühl in reinster Weise und hier muss auch die Geburtstätte eines neuen Stils gesucht werden.

Es ist diese Thatsache von grosser Wichtigkeit, um den materialistischen Unfug zu bekämpfen, der die architektonische Formgeschichte aus dem blossen Zwang des Materials, des Klimas, der Zwecke glaubt erklären zu müssen. Ich bin weit entfernt, die Bedeutung dieser Faktoren zu verkennen, muss aber doch daran festhalten, dass die eigentliche Formphantasie eines Volkes dadurch

---

[16] Seitdem wir die gegossenen Lettern unserer Druckschrift haben, ist freilich auch hier leichte Beweglichkeit verschwunden. Man hat sich heutzutage daran gewöhnt (in der üblichen Schrift) gotischen Minuskeln barocke Majuskeln vorzusetzen. Vgl. Bechstein, *Die deutsche Druckschrift*. 1885.

nicht in andere Bahnen gelenkt wird. Was ein Volk zu sagen hat, spricht es aus in jedem Fall und wenn wir seine Formensprache da beobachten, wo es zwanglos spricht und wir finden nachher in der grossen Kunst, in der Architektur, dieselben Formen wieder, dieselben Linien, dieselben Proportionen, so darf man von jener mechanischen Betrachtung wohl verlangen, dass sie verstumme.

Und damit hat der gefährlichste Gegner einer Kunstpsychologie das Feld geräumt.

Made in United States
North Haven, CT
27 May 2022

19533366R10075